"We struggle to know who we are outside of the roles, personality traits, or emotional scars we use to identify ourselves. Are we defined by the things we do or the things done to us? Who are we without our vocational wins, parenting successes, or individualistic giftings? In *Trading Faces*, John and Angel Beeson encourage us to look at who God is so that we can rightly see ourselves in light of our redemption and spiritual adoption. This book has stayed with me, reminding me that what matters most about me is who I am in Christ: I am *his*. Nothing brings more joy than that."

Glenna Marshall, author of *The Promise Is His Presence, Everyday Faithfulness*, and *Memorizing Scripture*

"*Trading Faces* is an important book for our cultural moment. John writes as an experienced pastor and Angel as a wise counselor. Together, they expose false identities, leading readers to Christ and the revolutionary new life he offers. John and Angel's work is biblical, honest, vulnerable, and worshipful. I believe it will help many find freedom and joy in Christ."

Kevin P. Halloran, author of *When Prayer Is a Struggle* and project manager for Open the Bible for Leaders

"Pastor John and Angel Beeson not only are theologically sound teachers but also bring a wealth of personal experience to this hard-hitting and transparent project. They speak with integrity and hearts of compassion. We heartily endorse this book."

Roger and Julie Barrier, Preach It, Teach It

"From the very first page, John and Angel speak to the things that roll around in my head every day. 'I'm a failure. I've blown it. I'm worthless. No matter what I accomplish, it's meaningless.' Then they speak to the one thing that makes sense of it all. I am an image bearer of God. How could God choose me to bear his image, to be like him? Then they unpack what that means for my life, and I begin to sense a change. This book is exactly what I need."

Tom Terry, author of *Like An Eagle*

"The author of Psalm 145 speaks of God's greatness as unsearchable. He doesn't mean we can't explore God's greatness, but rather that after we've searched and searched, there will always be more greatness to explore. We can speak of our identity in Christ in the same way. Yet Christians often don't know how much more there is for us in Christ, or how many false identities we wear, until someone shows us. John and Angel's book *Trading Faces* is a wonderful guide to exploring the unsearchable riches of our identity in Christ."

> Benjamin Vrbicek, lead pastor at Community Evangelical Free Church in Harrisburg, PA, managing editor for Gospel-Centered Discipleship, and author of several books

"John and Angel Beeson very skillfully unpack the difficult topic of our own identity. They do this in two ways: showing us how to ground our identity in Christ and contrasting our identity in Christ with substitute identities that we learn from our world. The Beesons give valuable evidence of their grasp of this topic through their own story and stories from the years of leading others in counseling and pastoral care. We live in a performative culture, catechized to put on masks to feel safe in this world. John and Angel gently help us remove them and find ourselves in Christ."

> John Starke, lead pastor at Apostles Church Uptown, New York, NY

"Solomon of old gives wisdom a personality, shapes an idea and gives it form, transforms words by giving them a voice: 'Wisdom calls out in the street; she makes her voice heard in the public squares. She cries out above the commotion; she speaks at the entrance of the city gates' (Prov. 1:20–21 CSB). This book stands in the line of such wisdom. As I read, I found myself beside a crackling fire, comforted by a soft chair, and felt my soul slowly breathe in long-desired rest—I was with friends. John and Angel's words weave together seamlessly and draw your attention to the only identity worth pursuing, the one you have in Jesus. This will remain a treasured book on my shelf, where it won't rest long."

> Chris Thomas, an Aussie, fellow follower of Jesus, imperfect pastor, and occasional blogger at *The Ploughman's Rest*

TRADING
FACES

TRADING
FACES

Removing the Masks That Hide
Your God-Given Identity

John & Angel Beeson

KREGEL
PUBLICATIONS

Cataloging-in-Publication data is available from the Library of Congress.

ISBN 978-0-8254-4784-6, print
ISBN 978-0-8254-7041-7, epub
ISBN 978-0-8254-6969-5, Kindle

Printed in the United States of America
23 24 25 26 27 28 29 30 31 / 5 4 3 2 1

To our children, Camille and Soren.
You are reflections of God's grace toward us.
As you know who you are in him, may you be
refreshed by his streams of living water.
We love you. He loves you.

Contents

CONTENTS

The Elusive Search

When I discover who I am, I'll be free.
—Ralph Ellison

One of the tragedies of our life is that we keep forgetting who we are.
—Henri Nouwen

JOHN

DANIEL DAY-LEWIS IS KNOWN AS one of the most committed method actors of our time. When he took on a role, he embodied the character not only on camera but off camera, and he only responded to his character's name. For the movie *In the Name of the Father*, Day-Lewis lost fifty pounds and spent three days in solitary confinement without water. For his role as a man with cerebral palsy who could only use his left foot, Day-Lewis lived like the character off-set, getting carried or wheelchaired, and was hand-fed all his meals. During the filming of *Gangs of New York*, which was set in nineteenth-century New York, Day-Lewis caught pneumonia because he insisted on wearing period-specific clothing. He then refused to take modern medicine and almost died as a result.[1]

"That is crazy!" we exclaim. And yet, many of us have spent our lives embodying roles that are not our true identities. We have lost track of what ultimate reality is.

Humans have been wearing emotional masks since we exited the garden of Eden. We try on identities, attempting to discover one where we find affirmation, peace, and security. We put on masks of vocation, role, and achievement, hoping to find the contentment we desperately long for.

No matter how many masks we put on, happiness eludes us. Rates of depression and suicide have never been higher. Marriages fail at alarming rates. More individuals in the United States have substance addictions than those who have cancer.[2] The happiness our masks promise remains out of reach for most.

How then can we find happiness? How can we be at peace? We believe the answer is found in two words: true identity.

Who Are You?

Wait a minute. Haven't we already tried to find happiness through identity?

In 1992, Robin Williams, voicing Genie, coaxed Aladdin, "Remember, be yourself." Nearly thirty years later, amid a culture steeped in a "be yourself" philosophy, we are more lost than ever. We've tried to be ourselves through our relationships, our careers, our parenting, our sexuality, and our patriotism. Genie's advice has failed. This isn't because we have neglected to live out the admonition but because we have never understood *who we are*. We have substituted false identities for our true identities.

As a counselor (Angel) and pastor (John), we've had hundreds of conversations with those who struggle to understand their purpose and find happiness. It's not surprising that few of those who are struggling can satisfactorily answer the most basic question: Who are you?

We invite you to stop right now. Don't read another word. Answer that question: Who are you? When you take off the masks, what is there? Write it in the margin or at the back of the book. We'll return to your answer later.

How We Talk to Ourselves

Modern science has confirmed the power of replacing negative self-talk with positive affirmations. Studies have shown that the practice of making daily affirmations decreases stress, increases the amount of time exercising, and may even lower the risk for cardiovascular disease.[3]

When Angel and I read these studies, we were surprised by the verifiable impact of positive self-affirmations. But we also question the way positive affirmations are taught and used. Our culture tells us to replace negative self-talk with affirmations based not in our identities in Christ but in our aspirations.

Secular therapists and coaches help clients recognize negative self-talk. You might identify with some of these thoughts:

- "I'm so ugly."
- "I'll always be fat."
- "I'll never get a promotion."
- "I hate myself."
- "I'm such a loser."
- "This is going to fail."
- "Everyone leaves me out."
- "No one thinks I can do this."
- "I am the problem."
- "I am dirty."

According to these therapists and coaches, the next step is to replace this harmful self-talk with positive statements. Those statements might look like the following:

- "I am beautiful."
- "I enjoy exercising."
- "I will create opportunities for myself."
- "I love who I am."
- "I am successful."
- "I love defying the odds."
- "I am valued."
- "I believe in myself."

Cruise down the self-help aisle in Barnes & Noble and you'll be sure to find a title promising you that your life will be changed by actualizing your effervescent, perfectly capable self.

Does that make anyone else uncomfortable? Angel and I are allergic to this model of positive self-talk. Why? Because it is not grounded in our identity in Christ but rather in the shifting sand of our own thoughts and beliefs. We can say "I love who I am" a million times in a mirror, but if it's rooted in our self-belief, the first time we see something about ourselves we want to change, we'll topple. And what happens when real gusts of hardship come? What happens when life inevitably proves we are not the masters of our lives, in control of all circumstances?

And yet, while the secular therapists who have researched and promoted self-affirmation have built their practice on too weak a foundation, their methods are worth considering. Not only does science support positive thinking, but Scripture also asks us to affirm our identities. It is no accident that the New Testament writers make direct statements of truth about themselves and their readers. It is not enough for the truths of our identities in Christ to be passively received, like a child might memorize a list of United States presidents or states to simply say they know who they are or where they are located. Is naming them enough? It isn't what we know; it is what we do with what we know. Therein lies the power. Affirmations have purpose. If God's voice of truth in Scripture speaks a word about us, then we are invited to speak it over ourselves.

In fact, God encourages us to speak his truths over ourselves. Paul likens this to putting on a new article of clothing: Christ himself (Rom. 13:14; Gal. 3:27). When we put on our "new self" (Col. 3:10), we put on the likeness of Christ and his virtues, and we take off the "old self" (Col. 3:9). But we don't just put on Christ; we are also to put away the falsehoods (Eph. 4:25) that the Enemy has taught us to repeat.

Far too many Christians have let the Enemy have a foothold in their lives under the deception that negative self-talk is somehow godlier. When we speak poorly about ourselves, we can feel like we're being humble. It is true that we are sinners in desperate need of a Savior. It is true that secular positive affirmations are vacuous if they are built on our personal ability to make them come to pass. But when we open the Bible, we see that it is full of affirmations far better than our culture provides.

Consider how replete the Bible is with statements of profound worth. Echoing God's Word, we can say with confidence:

- "I am wonderfully made."
- "I am adopted by the perfect Father."
- "I am beloved."
- "I am a conqueror."
- "I am God's friend."
- "I am protected."
- "I am pure."
- "I am a saint."
- "I am God's treasure."
- "I am gifted."
- "We are God's beautiful bride."
- "We are the light of the world."

- "We are unified."
- "We are his temple."
- "He will complete his good work through me."

It is a good thing to start and finish our day with these statements of biblical affirmation. If we trust in the words of Scripture, then believing these statements and letting them form our hearts and shape our self-talk will grow us into the likeness of Christ in a powerful way. If the King of Kings and Lord of Lords calls us valuable, then we can absolutely believe and say we are valuable. Biblical affirmations make much of God's voice over us. As we navigate forward, we pray that you hear more of your Master's voice and less of the false voices we all naturally tend to amplify.

Substitute Identities

I am not much of a baker (Angel, on the other hand, is fantastic). Some years ago, I tried to surprise my family with a Saturday morning breakfast. Picture the scene: Angel and the kids are asleep, the weekend rain pitter-patters on the roof, and a family breakfast seems to be the perfect way to start the lazy day.

Homemade biscuits sound like the ideal complement to my standard eggs and bacon. I thumb through our recipe book and pull out Angel's family biscuit recipe. "Two cups flour. Got it. Three-quarters teaspoon salt. Check." I pour the Morton's into the teaspoon and flip it over into the bowl. "Two and a half teaspoons baking powder. Hmm . . . where did that baking powder go? Where did it go?" Cupboards open and close. Nope. "Ahhh . . . well, here's baking soda. Almost, but not quite. Baking powder, where are you?"

I stand back and consider my options. Do I wake Angel up? No. Any hope of brownie points would evaporate. Do I run to the store? No, sir. What if the kids wake up while I'm away? Lazy Saturday morning ruined. How similar are baking soda and baking powder? They've got to be pretty similar, right? And in the baking soda goes.

The fork scrapes the bowl as the biscuits are mixed. The coffee is ground and percolated. The bacon sizzles in the pan, and the eggs are salted, peppered, and scrambled. I dollop the biscuit dough out onto the pan and put them into the oven.

The smell of breakfast fills our home, and Camille, Soren, and Angel file into the kitchen, give me a thank-you hug, and pile breakfast onto their plates. We sit. We give thanks.

Then from the kitchen table, the first bite of biscuit is taken. "Gross! What did you do to the biscuits, Daddy?"

Uh-oh. I take a bite. It tastes metallic and soapy. Yuck! It turns out baking soda is not a perfect substitute for baking powder.

Many of us put substitute ingredients in place of the true ingredients of our identity. Seems like they should work, but those substitute identities will leave us as disappointed as baking soda in biscuits.

Labels, Roles, and Identity

So, who are you? Many respond to that question by sharing their roles: "I am a mom." "I am a dad." "I am a sister." "I am a wife." "I am a husband." "I am a lawyer." "I am a teacher." "I am an athlete."

It's not surprising that we answer the question this way. One of the first questions we ask children is "What do you want to be when you grow up?" It's a fine question, but by asking it over and over again, we teach kids that they are what they do. We coach our children to substitute roles for true identities.

Angel grew up with a mission to be a wife. She planned her wedding in fourth grade. She started praying for her future husband in sixth grade. In hindsight, she admits she was setting herself up for failure. Everything she did was to craft her identity around being a wife. She had a false understanding of her true north. It led to a season of fighting for her own happiness and escape. When her identity as a wife imploded, she tried out her identity as a health nut, a yogi, and a photographer. None of those identities satisfied her. Eventually she went after other men. She thought that perhaps they would make her feel beautiful and worth something. Adultery and death were at her doorstep. Her world turned upside down, and every childhood holy pursuit was now a reflection of self-hatred and condemnation. She came face-to-face with her own internal desperation before a living God. She had failed in her identity as a wife and mom. Little did she know, Jesus had way more to say about her. Jesus took her brokenness and then put her back together. Only when she found her identity in Jesus could she experience his wholeness.

As youngsters grow into teenagers and teenagers into young adults, it is more likely that roles become substitute identities. The amorphous blob of elementary children separates into distinct groups—the geeks, jocks, thespians, musicians, punks, emo kids, mean girls, preps, and church kids. What teenage movie doesn't riff on the interplay among these groups? Despite what they say, every teen longs to embody a label. We want to be able to make sense of who we are and where we fit in this world.

As youngsters grow into teenagers and teenagers into young adults, it is more likely that roles become substitute identities.

I remember one summer when my parents took our family to a one-week camp in New Mexico. During the day, we divided into our respective age groups. I went off with the eleven- and twelve-year-olds. We gathered in a gazebo and introduced ourselves. As introductions began, a light bulb went off in my head. "No one knows me here! I can be whoever I want to be." My turn came and I introduced myself as "Johnny." None of my friends back home called me Johnny.

But maybe this was the moment to break through to a new, cooler me. I didn't just go by a different name; I tried on a new personality. I acted tougher and more aloof. Tough-guy "Johnny" was a fraud, so at night I had to keep my family away from my new friends. I feared my parents would discover my duplicity. I was Johnny by day, John by night, slipping on the personalities like sweatshirts. I was relieved when we pulled away from the camp and I bid farewell to "Johnny." The charade was over, and I was grateful.

The hunt for our identity doesn't stop as adults. We latch onto identifiers. We join Facebook pages, read books and blogs, join clubs, and make friends with those who are like-minded. We hunt for those like us. When we learn someone else has the same quirky tastes, we light up. The two of us appreciate undiscovered music and strategy board games. When we find someone similar, we think, "You're one of us!"

And so we identify ourselves by family, marriage, vocation, political party, style, where we grew up or where we live, even by the grocery store we frequent. (Can we get an "Amen," fellow Trader Joe's loyalists?)

Sexual preferences are another means of creating identity. It's not surprising that our culture has become obsessed with gender. Because some group identities are formed based on sexual preferences, there is a push to label those preferences earlier and earlier. It makes sense (from the world's perspective) that if our identity is found in our sexual preferences, then we would want children to identify their sexual preferences as early as possible. Similarly, we are dissatisfied with binary genders, desiring subsets ad infinitum because we think they can express our identity. Yet such answers are found wanting, just like all the rest.

Substitutes, all.

Our preferences do not define who we are. They are not ultimate. Our roles do not define who we are. In fact, every one of our roles can change. For us, if one of us dies, we will shift from spouse to widow or widower. If we change careers or retire, we will no longer be a pastor or a counselor.

We assert that making our vocations, our families, our independence, our personalities, or our righteousness into our identities will not sustain us. We will deal with each of these issues in the chapters that follow.

God has given you valuable roles. But don't confuse them with your identity. They make poor substitutes that will not satisfy.

Who you are in Christ is unchangeable and nonnegotiable. If and when you experience the transforming work of Christ in your life, you are given new identities that cannot change. Christ offers us multifaceted identities in him. In him we are saints, sons, servants, and much more. Coming to grips with these true identities brings about holistic peace and radical freedom.

To answer the question "Who am I?" is to set the true north of your life. Understanding that your true identities are in Christ allows you to step into being who you were made to be and living how you were designed to live.

An Identity Built on Sand

To begin grappling with the depth of who you truly are, you will need to allow some aspects of how you view yourself to shift from being things that define you to things that express you. Roles, achievements, pursuits, and so on can be good, but they should not be foundational.

As God's image bearers, we need to let the old pass away; we were made for more. When Paul writes to the church at Corinth, he invites them into a new freedom, which comes as we behold who God is and allow him to transform our identities. "Now the Lord is the Spirit, and where the Spirit of the Lord is, there is freedom. And we all, with unveiled face, beholding the glory of the Lord, are being transformed into the same image from one degree of glory to another" (2 Cor. 3:17–18). When we encounter God, he changes us into who he has made us to be. We trade our earthbound faces for his ultimate identities for us. A door is important, but it cannot substitute for a foundation.

Our circumstances are not our fundamental flaw or problem. Our anxiety and depression do not define us; nor do our marital, financial, relational, sexual, or vocational issues. Our circumstances are not who we are.

When we define ourselves by our roles, our preferences, or our situations, we have built our identity on a foundation of sand.

Not long ago, Angel and I took a work vacation to Tijuana, Mexico, in order to be intentional with our writing projects. On the beach was a stretch of homes built on the cliffs—idyllic, but not reinforced with steel and concrete. Year after year, the tide has drawn the sand from the cliffs into the sea. Grain by grain, the cliffs have inched back. Some homes have already slid down the sea-worn banks. Others hang precariously over the edge with foundations exposed. It is only a matter of time until they join the fate of the other poorly anchored homes. So it is with our lives: when we've built our identity on what the world whispers to us about who we are rather than on the solid truths of who God declares us to be, we soon find that our exposed foundations prove unsupportive.

Our Battles

It took both of us a long time to fully understand who we are in Christ and then to root our lives in that identity. We will share some of those battles in the pages that follow.

As a counselor and a pastor, Angel and I walk with those who are engaged in these battles every day. We witness the struggles to understand identities. They are real. Every person reading this book has a unique story with unique trials. Scars tell the stories of battles won and lost. They speak of trauma and abuse; they speak of broken homes; they speak of doubt; they speak of addiction.

But hear this: there is hope for you. You might not see even a flicker of hope today, but your Creator does. Your Savior does. Can you trust the One who knit you together in the beginning of time—trust him enough to believe that what he sees in you is more trustworthy than what you see in yourself?

Is it hard to fully live into the identity Christ has purposed for us? Yes, it does not come naturally. Have you ever noticed how dogs swim? Most dogs look unnatural in the water. Their heads point awkwardly out of the water; their legs, perfectly designed for running and jumping on land, look silly paddling along. Now consider the dolphin: a flick of its tail propels it through the water effortlessly, and it changes course at angles that don't seem possible. When it comes to living in the reality of our true identity, many of us are more like dogs in water than dolphins. Even though we've been told we belong in the water, we struggle to put our heads under and really live as God has called us.

Pastor Eugene Peterson reminds us, "Identity does not begin when I begin to understand myself. There is something previous to what I think about myself, and it is what God thinks of me. That means that everything I think and feel is by nature a response, and the one to whom I respond is God. I never speak the first word. I never make the first move."[4] Let's let God speak the first word to us; let's let God make the first move. When we trust his promises more than what our hearts tell us, and when we trust his true north over our culture's, then we will begin to feel and live differently.

We believe that most struggles are fundamentally struggles with identity. The only way to experience the peace, contentment, and joy for which God has made us is to understand who we truly are.

Let's journey together. Angel and I hope to help you navigate both the breadth and depth of your true identity in Christ. To do so, we will examine ten substitute identities that masquerade as true identities. As we consider each of these identities together, we will challenge you to take off the mask of that false identity and exchange it for a true identity that Christ gives to those who trust him.

The only way to experience the peace, contentment, and joy for which God has made us is to understand who we truly are.

We pray that God uses these words to accomplish his transformative purpose in your heart. We invite you to move forward with us. May you taste and see that the Lord is good, and may you believe his Word about who you are.

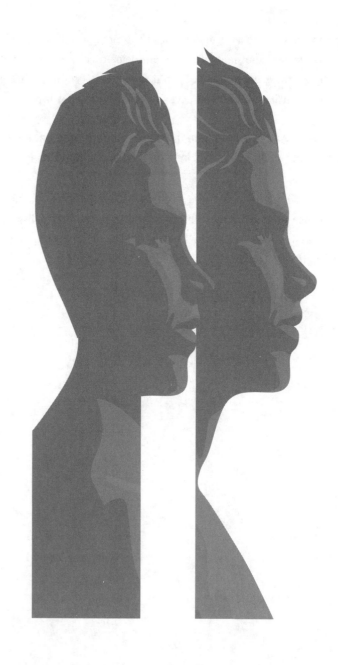

Shame
Finding Worth as an Image Bearer

—

The shame that tormented me was all the more corrosive for having no very clear origin: I didn't know why I felt so tainted, and worthless, and wrong—only that I did, and whenever I looked up from my books I was swamped by slimy waters rushing in from all sides.
—Donna Tartt, *The Goldfinch*

Humanity is a plague. We're a disgusting, narcissistic, selfish parasite, and the world would be a better place without us.
—Tony, as played by Ricky Gervais in *After Life*

You have made them a kingdom and priests to our God, and they shall reign on the earth.
—the twenty-four elders in the book of Revelation

ANGEL

I SIT WITH A YOUNG woman. She exhales and looks at her shoes. "My grandfather molested me when I was six. My father first raped me when I was eleven. Abusive boyfriends took his place by the time I was thirteen. Alcohol, drugs, men. It's been the story of my life." She looks up at me flatly. "Nothing works. I hate myself. I am worthless."

John got the call from Brian's mother this morning. "He committed suicide last night." John's heart drops and he remembers their last session. "My kids would be better off without me," he said. "My wife has moved on. She already has a boyfriend. She won't even look me in the eye." Brian made assurances that he would not commit suicide. But as he sat in his truck pulled off to the side of the road, looking at the home he had been forced to sell when he and his wife separated, his emotions probably churned inside of him. He might have remembered the first day they moved in, with all their hopes and aspirations. His thoughts may have drifted to teaching his kids how to ride their bikes, to a fight he and his wife had, to a piñata hung up on a mesquite tree for a birthday party. And in the end, he believed the world was a better place without him.

The American Psychological Association reports that suicide rates have increased 30 percent in the past two decades.[1] In the age group of fifteen- to twenty-four-year-olds, the rate of increase is a staggering 56 percent.[2]

How can self-hatred be so pervasive in this age of self-positivity?

The rise of suicide rates has directly correlated with the rise of social media.[3] John and I don't think that is a coincidence. Never in the history of the world has there been a time when we all are more susceptible to the dangerous trap of comparison.

When we grew up, we compared ourselves with classmates and neighbors. Today, via social media, we compare ourselves to virtually any acquaintance we've ever had. And that comparison is poisonous. No matter how great our lives might be, one glance on social media is sure to remind us that someone out there has a better life than we do. A discouraging day is compounded by social media, where we are sure to see friends in some exotic location.

The Voice of Shame

Many of us live with a voice that speaks words of despair into our ears: "I am a fraud." "I am so messed up." "I am stupid." "I am pathetic." "I am worthless." And the you messages: "You suck." "Everyone knows you're an idiot." "Who do you think you are?" "Everyone thinks you are such a loser." "No one will ever want you."

This shame attendant has been present since the relationship between humans and God ruptured. One of the reasons we feel shame is because God has an enemy (and therefore we do too!). His name is Satan, and he's the accuser and tempter of human beings. Shame is Satan's most powerful tool to estrange us from God and to multiply the power of sin in our lives. When Adam and Eve rejected God's authority in their lives and chose to eat of the Tree of Knowledge of Good and Evil, what was their immediate response? Shame. Suddenly aware of their nakedness, they hid their bodies. Guilty of what they had done and ashamed of who they were, they hid from their Maker.

This is what shame does: it alienates us from one another and from God. While guilt is our response to what we have done, shame tells us that we *are* what we have done. Gripped with the fear of what we will see if we encounter ourselves, we hide from ourselves, others, and God.

The voice of shame records fragments of conversations with others that echo our worst fears about ourselves and plays them on a loop. John has told me horror stories of the many times he's heard, in the chambers of his heart, the echo of an elder's words at a church he pastored: "You are unfit for ministry." The context of that statement is wiped out; John's heart ignores how he's changed since then. Instead, he feels the words aimed like a bony finger at his chest, accusing him, defeating him.

The voice of shame records fragments of conversations that echo our worst fears about ourselves and plays them on a loop.

The voice of shame also takes even small events and attaches messages to them. We write a text message to a friend that is reciprocated with silence. "You aren't worth his time," the voice tells us. Yesterday John spoke to a group of pastors, and no one followed up with a text or email. "You should have declined the invitation to speak. Now they know you are an imposter."

It happens in anticipation as well. Invited to speak to a group of pastors, I have heard the voice of shame speak to me: "You're stupid. What do you have to offer these older, wiser men?" The voice speaks to us both as we write this book: "Who do you think you are? You're not authors. No one will read this."

Once Satan instigates shame, he hands us fraudulent tools to escape its imprisonment: comparison, comfort, and numbing.

"If you just compare yourselves to others who are worse, you will feel better," he lies. "Console yourself with this bowl of ice cream," he coos. "Ease your pain with this porn," he entices. "Shut down so you don't have to feel these bad feelings," he whispers.

The shame attendant rubs his hands together when we cave to comparison, comfort, and numbing. Scrolling social media creates more fodder for shame, as does the bowl of ice cream, masturbation, and numbing. Shame wants us to stop, to freeze, to shrink.

Our flesh goes to great lengths to avoid pain and seek comfort. The danger and irony of shame language is that it arrogantly dismisses God. Shame plugs our ears from hearing the voice of God and refuses his truth about who we are.

Amplifying the voice of shame can feel as though we are acting in humility. But it is not humble to believe lies. It is not humble to reject what God says about us. It is sinful to deny God's words over us; when we do, we position ourselves on the enemy's battlefield in allegiance with him.

How do we break the cycle of shame? How do we fight the voice that tells us we are worthless?

The First Word

To shut down the lies of shame, we must open our ears to the truth God speaks to us. The first word on who we are in the Bible is a word that speaks to our incredible value. In the first chapter of the first book of the Bible, Genesis 1, the story of creation is laid out before us. As God creates the cosmos, he revels in its beauty and perfection. Punctuating each of God's creations is God's delight in his creation: "God saw that it was good." Stars and planets, saguaros and palm trees, centipedes and elephants . . . God smiles and laughs. "Good, good, good!"

But God is not finished. The stage is set, but the lead actors are not in place.

> Then God said, "Let us make man in our image, after our
> likeness. And let them have dominion over the fish of the
> sea and over the birds of the heavens and over the livestock

and over all the earth and over every creeping thing that creeps on the earth."

So God created man in his own image,
in the image of God he created him;
male and female he created them. (vv. 26–27)

As a human being, you hold the unique distinction of bearing the image of the Almighty, the Creator. You were created in God's image. You have permission to declare with confidence, "Hi, my name is [fill in the blank], and I am an image bearer of God Almighty!" This is true. "I am worthless" is a lie. Receiving our identity as an image bearer of God gives us permission to be freed from the prison of shame.

We are invited to look into the mirror of God himself—not the mirror of our expectations, not the mirror of society or media, not the mirror of family, friends, and acquaintances—and see that God says we are "very good" (v. 31). God's first word about all of us is that we are good.

When you look in the mirror with disdain, when you hate how you look or that you're not smart enough, you are not speaking of who you are—you are speaking of who God is. Self-hatred is God-hatred.

The story of the creation of Adam and Eve concludes with these words: "And the man and his wife were both naked and were not ashamed" (2:25). God made you to be naked and unashamed. Author Curt Thompson writes that shame "wants to destroy everything about the world that God intended for goodness and beauty."[4] One day, free of sin and with the shame attendant's voice banished to hell, you will experience the glory of a life free of shame.

A Masterpiece?

Who is your favorite artist? Da Vinci? Van Gogh? Picasso? Imagine that a benefactor gave you one of their masterpieces. In your living room hangs Da Vinci's *Mona Lisa*, or Van Gogh's *Starry Night*, or Picasso's *Les Demoiselles D'Avignon*. You invite a friend over for dinner. You welcome him at the door, and he steps into your living room. His eyes squint and his nose turns up. "What's that ugly piece of trash?" he says.

What is your response? Do you take your friend seriously? Have you misjudged the work of art? Or do you recognize that while you have a masterpiece, you also have a friend with poor judgment?

You were created by *the* Master Artist. Better than Da Vinci's *Mona Lisa*, better than Van Gogh's *Starry Night*, better than Picasso's *Les Demoiselles D'Avignon*, are *you*, the masterpiece of the Master Artist. So when you look in the mirror and think awful things about who you are, your inner voice is acting like that imaginary friend who criticized the masterpiece in your living room.

Our self-hatred speaks of our misjudgment, not of the flawed artistry of the Master Artist. God looks at you, his masterpiece, and says, "You are very good!" He's not a liar.

Not only are you God's masterpiece, but Genesis 1:27 says you are made in his image. What does it mean for you to image God? There are three primary ways you do so. First, you image God's *attributes*. Second, you image God's *relationality*. Third, you image God's *reign*.

You Image God's Attributes

You image the attributes of the one true God. The Bible tells us those attributes include God's

- holiness (Isa. 6:1–8)
- goodness (Ps. 34:8)
- justice (Jer. 23:5)
- love (1 John 4:7–19)
- grace (John 1:17)
- mercy (Ps. 103)

- faithfulness (2 Tim. 2:13)
- wisdom (James 1:5–6)
- freedom (Exod. 3:14)
- beauty (Ps. 27:4)

Each of these attributes is reflected in you. Go through each characteristic and ask whether you can see it in yourself. (If you're not sure what a word means, or even if you think you know, look it up in a dictionary or Google it.) Can you see God's mercy in you? His goodness? His justice? Wherever you see these attributes, you see the reflection of the Master Artist in you.

In *The Help*, the maid Aibileen Clark speaks a blessing over the child she is caring for: "You is kind. You is smart. You is important."[5] That's what God says about *you*. When he sees you, he sees his own attributes and image reflected in you.

When you resist the temptation to finish the Ben and Jerry's pint to numb your pain, God sees his holiness in you.

When you do what is right and claim tips on your taxes, God sees his goodness in you.

When you use your voice for someone mistreated, God sees his justice in you.

When you cradle your colicky newborn, God sees his love in you.

When you offer forgiveness to your friend who gossiped about you, God sees his grace in you.

When you release someone from a debt, God sees his mercy in you.

When you choose to go to counseling to preserve your marriage, God sees his faithfulness in you.

When you say no to entertainment because of a looming test, God sees his wisdom in you.

When you refuse to engage in crude joking, God sees his freedom
in you.

When your joyful laugh fills a room, God sees his beauty in you.

You were made to reflect the attributes of God to a world desperately in need of them. In a world that aches for justice, truth,
love, mercy, and beauty, God has placed you to magnify his perfect
attributes.

You Image God's Relationality

Christianity claims that God is triune. The word *triune* means that
the one true God has existed eternally in perfect relational unity:
the Father, the Son, and the Holy Spirit. As human beings created in
God's image, we display all the three persons of the Trinity: the Father, Son, and Holy Spirit. We also reflect their triune relationship.

The Father says you were fashioned perfectly from the beginning. You were formed in secret. Woven in the depths of the earth.
The Father says he saw your unformed substance and wrote in the
book of life every one of your days (Ps. 139:15–16).

The Son died so his blood could make you right before him. The
Son, who knew no sin, became sin, so you could be made righteous
(2 Cor. 5:21). Jesus looks upon you as the "joy that was set before
him" (Heb. 12:2) on his road to Golgotha.

The Holy Spirit dwells intimately in you so that not only do you
have a helper 24-7, but you can also be made alive and go forth in
the power of his name (Rom. 8:11).

As image bearers, we reflect the relationality of our triune God.
From eternity, God is in community. And he makes us for community. In Ephesians 2, Paul explains that those who have trusted
Christ have been saved by grace through faith and then brought
into community through the peace of Christ. He concludes that we

"are being built together into a dwelling place for God by the Spirit" (v. 22). We display who God is when we are together. He made us for one another, and as we love one another and are united in heart and mind, we reflect his triune character.

You Image God's Reign

Dominion.

If you take a look at the verses we quoted on pages 29–30 about the creation of mankind, you'll see that *dominion* is the first word about how you reflect God's image. You are the image bearer of the high King of Kings, intended to "have dominion over" (we will return to this theme in greater depth in chapter 9). Having dominion means God gives us authority to oversee, nurture, and steward that which he has given us responsibility for. You are set apart from creation and intended for a higher purpose. You are the unique and beautiful actor God created for his stage to reflect himself.

The first way we reflect God's image is by reflecting his benevolent rule on earth: we reign, but we do so in a way that's best for everyone.

We live out dominion in our workplaces, in parenting, over finances, in the kitchen, and in our neighborhoods. When we are employees who work hard, are filled with integrity, and treat people in front of us as fellow image bearers of God, we practice dominion as God intended. As we discipline our children in unity, mercy, and grace, we display God's dominion. Dominion can be shared. In marriage, when we jointly make purchasing, banking, and budgeting decisions, we demonstrate dominion. When we collaboratively cook a delicious meal, we steward God's gift of cuisine. As we open our home in hospitality to our neighbors, we exercise dominion in the place we live.

One of John's and my favorite shared things to do is to practice dominion in the space God has given us. We love stepping outside to cultivate our yard into a place of beauty. We dig the soil, pot a plant, pick weeds, and prune trees. As we work, we inhale gratitude and exhale prayers of surrender. "It is good," we tell our King as we care for his garden.

Humans were made for dominion. We are servants who have been given talents (giftings, finances, and opportunities) from our Master with a call to steward them for his glory (Matt. 25:14–30). It is life giving when we understand who we are and give ourselves permission to see ourselves from God's point of view.

You are made to reign and reflect his kind rule. You are his king. You are his queen.

The Last Word

God undoes shame not just with his first word about us from creation but also with his last word on the cross.

"It is finished," Jesus declares in his final moments. On the cross Jesus speaks the last word to shame as he identifies with our shame and removes its power. The Enemy's whispers of shame are silenced as Jesus purchases us with his blood. Our sin—rejecting God in thought, word, or action—doesn't define us; his acceptance of us does. The sinless man becomes sin that we might be freed from sin. The unshameable man becomes shame that we might be freed from shame. Like the sponge he's given to drink from, Jesus is saturated in sin and shame. The shaming of the perfect man undoes shame.

Satan went into his bag of tricks and pulled out the most powerful one he had: shame. It was a ploy that had proved effective time and time again. He must have howled in delight to use it on the very Son of God.

God undoes shame on Good Friday. The story of the cross is not merely the story of guilt being removed but of shame being undone.

The Romans devised crucifixion not just to torture those they killed but also to inflict shame in the process. The victim hung completely naked on the torture device, arms outstretched and unable to cover himself.[6]

> **The story of the cross is not merely the story of guilt being removed but of shame being undone.**

On the cross, Christ makes atonement for our sin. The penalty is paid by the blood of the God-man poured out on the cross. But the work of Christ does not end there; Jesus takes the full sting of shame on the cross and removes its poison.

Christ's arrest begins with a kiss by one of his closest friends, an act of respect and intimacy used to bring the shame of betrayal. He is abandoned by all but two of his friends: more shame. One of his closest friends then denies him: additional shame. The spiritual authorities place him on a bogus trial: shameful. The political authorities put him on trial: shame. The crowds turn against Christ, mocking him, begging for an insurrectionist to be released instead of him and demanding his crucifixion: shame multiplies. He is stripped naked, mocked as king, and spat upon: shame deepens. Through a crowd, he drags a cross to Golgotha and is hung between two enemies of the state who also mock him: shame mounts. He hangs naked as the soldiers gamble for his clothing: shame. He cries out to God, publicly expressing his hurt, fear, and forsakenness: shame culminates.

On the road to the cross, Jesus walks into the heart of shame. He has plunged deeper into shame than we could ever imagine and has destroyed the Enemy's weapon of shame. Just as Christ absorbed our sin on the cross, he also absorbs our shame. Satan will seek to destroy us through shame, but because of the cross, that shame is a lie and has no ultimate power. Satan will attack, but "no weapon that is fashioned against you shall succeed" (Isa. 54:17). We can walk the path as image bearers without shame because Jesus, the perfect image bearer, has already walked the path of shame for us on the cross.

Jesus knows the shame you have experienced. Because he has walked its path, you are no longer bound by its lies. Dane Ortlund frames this explosive truth this way: "That God is rich in mercy means that your regions of deepest shame and regret are not hotels through which divine mercy passes but homes in which divine mercy abides. It means the things about you that make you cringe most, make him hug hardest."[7] The cross reveals the heart of God. God is not repulsed by our shame. The Merciful One knows you and loves you.

You are not worthless. You bear the image of the almighty God, the creator of the universe. The cross of Christ speaks of your worth. You are worth the life of the very Son of God, Jesus.

When we open our ears to hear the voice of God, the voice of shame is silenced. When we hear God speak his truth over our lives, we step out of patterns of comparison, self-comfort, and numbing, and we move forward in his love. Psychologist Curt Thompson says, "Where shame attempts to push us into static inertia, love bids us to *move*."[8]

Shame tries to steal the pen from the great Author and rewrite his stories in our lives. Let God take back the pen of your story. God authors a story "of hope and creativity, one that scorns shame in order to imagine new minds, new possibilities and new narratives."[9] Step into God's kingdom story as his image bearer, and live in the power and truth of his words over you, words he has spoken from creation and from the cross. Will you receive them? Make a choice today to trust him. Make a choice today to die to a false self.

Make a choice to take off any jersey that would name you with self-condemnation and put on a jersey that speaks God's truth: you are worthy, redeemed, holy, beautiful, valuable, loved, and established.

PRAYER

Father, forgive me for so easily dismissing you and who you say I am. I bear your image. Forgive me for listening to the lies of shame. I receive the gift of Jesus on the cross, who took my shame and set me free from its burden. Jesus, your blood purifies me. Forgive me for the lies I speak over myself. Forgive me for the ways in which I condemn myself. Lord, I repent of the specific lies shame has convinced me are true. I am not stupid. I am not ugly. I am not a loser. I am not worthless. You say I am worthy, I am redeemed, I am holy, I am beautiful, I am valuable, I am loved, and I am established. I receive your truth for myself. Teach me to hear your voice. Teach me to be satisfied in you, holy God. Teach me to trust whatever you call me into today. You anoint, equip, and empower me to be who I am. I am yours. Thank you that I can walk in the blessing of being made in your image and say, with you, that it is very good. Amen.

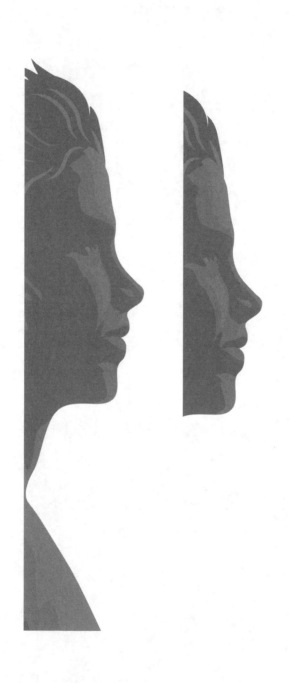

Good Works
Finding Acceptance as a Redeemed Sinner

The most fearful punishment of sinners is simply to leave them to themselves.
—Thomas Moore

Christianity begins with the doctrine of sin.
—Søren Kierkegaard

Sin is not wrongdoing; it is wrong being; deliberate and emphatic independence of God.
—Oswald Chambers

JOHN

REBECCA'S PARENTS WERE GOOD PEOPLE, but the unintentional expectations they laid on her created a grid of self-worth that was finally starting to crumble. She was a standout student, accomplished in her career, and now she was trying to be the perfect wife and mom. But the weight of the internal demands was crushing her. Angel coaxed her to put in words what those demands were, and bit by bit they leaked out. She finally concluded, "I'm so tired of trying to be good. Everyone expects so much of me. I expect so much of me. But I can't keep it up."

Caleb had an uncanny ability to remember names and lit up when he saw a familiar face come in the room. It all seemed so genuine and effortless . . . until it wasn't. His outgoing personality was a crumbling façade hiding the pain and addictions in his life. Now he looked shell-shocked. He shared, "She found out last week that I've been addicted to porn since we've been married, and that I've been hiding the fact that I sometimes smoke pot. I don't know how to keep it up otherwise. People expect so much of me. I don't know how to calm my needs and my anxieties otherwise."

How do you measure how good you are? I don't mean the unchanging image-bearer goodness we discussed in the previous chapter. I'm referring to your assessment of your own moral character. My guess is that you have your ways of measuring yourself. We all keep tabs on how virtuous we are.

It's true. I keep score. I measure my goodness by the fact that I always put the shopping cart back in the corral, and I never litter. (Well, not on purpose.)

We devise manifold ways to judge how good we are. Usually they involve comparing ourselves against others. From parenting to political allegiance to what grocery store we shop at, we create all sorts of ways to judge and validate ourselves.

Our secular world pretends it has done away with the moral trappings of objective right and wrong. Yet, ironically, it is obsessed with righteousness (what is right or justified). In *Seculosity*, David Zahl, a popular theologian and culture critic, argues that the contemporary world has transmuted the religious desire for righteousness into markers that we can judge. Our secular world multiplies its demand for our performance. Zahl explains, "Performancism is the assumption, usually unspoken, that there is no distinction between what we *do* and who we *are*. Your resumé isn't part of your identity; it *is* your identity."[1]

Piety, holiness, and righteousness aren't merely in the domain of religion. Our hearts long to be known as good. The question is, What piety will we run after? Zahl says,

> Listen carefully and you'll hear that word *enough* everywhere, especially when it comes to the anxiety, loneliness, exhaustion, and division that plague our moment to such tragic proportions. You'll hear about people scrambling to be successful enough, happy enough, thin enough, wealthy enough, influential enough, desired enough, charitable enough, woke enough, *good* enough. We believe instinctively that, were we to reach some benchmark in our minds, then value, vindication, and love would be ours—that if we got enough, we would *be* enough.[2]

What are the benchmarks in your life that you use to measure how good you are? Your grades? A number on the bathroom scale? Your salary? Your title? The number of Twitter followers you have? That person you constantly compare yourself to?

The truth about the flesh (who we are after Adam and Eve's rebellion against God, selfish and sin-directed) is that it is never satisfied. It's like a coyote: No matter how much you feed it, it stays hungry. If food is scarce, these wild animals will hunt until they find anything, even if it means the puppy in your backyard. Coyotes are creatures of the flesh, always on the prowl for more to devour. Our flesh is the same. It hungers but is never satisfied; it is always in need of more. We desire more and more. The number on the scale goes lower. The salary goes higher.

Worse still, we feel the need to be justified in the world's eyes. We long for validation. But we can never be good enough. We might feel better than some, but in our heart of hearts, while we all desperately want to be enough, we know that we aren't.

Bad News

At the end of the 2019 biopic about Elton John, *Rocketman*, the child Reggie Dwight (Elton's given name) looks to himself as a grown-up and asks, "Well, when are you going to hug me?"[3] Richard Dexter, the movie's director, frames Elton John's story as one of the rock star dealing with wounds he was dealt as a child, moving from cycles of self-destruction to self-love.

Every one of us knows something is wrong within us. We struggle with finding and experiencing true love. We grapple with an inner sense of woundedness and longing for connection and acceptance. Elton John's story resonates because each of us has a child within that is asking, "Well, when are you going to hug me?"

We all long to be held. We long to be known and loved.

How do we attain that love and acceptance? The world tells us that, as with Elton John, ours is a journey of self-acceptance, of believing we are good enough. However, the Bible gives us a very different perspective on that journey. It doesn't shy away from the hard news that, ever since the fall, the natural bent of our hearts is toward sin. The Bible tells us that, on our own, we really are *not* good enough. On our own, we are sinners.

That sure sounds like bad news, and our world doesn't deal well with bad news. We throw everything we've got at stopping the aging process. We skirt conversations about depression, failure, and death. We look to successes, to actors and athletes and business moguls, for their secrets.

You can go online today and get swag galore that speaks of your worth: "I am confident," "Hello, beautiful," "I am worthy," "I can, I will," "I am enough," "Gorgeous," and on and on. Now, all these statements *can* be true about us—but we can't circumvent how they *become* true because they aren't fully true until we have been transformed by Christ.

We can't get to the good news without coming to grips with the bad news.

Without Christ

Released during the positivity and self-esteem movement, Radiohead's song "Creep" voiced the inner fears of the first contemporary generation that had grown up on affirmation and participation trophies.

In his haunting, neurotic voice, Thom Yorke expresses the ruminations and fears of all of us. He longs for a perfect body and soul. He wishes he was special and craves attention. But in his heart of hearts, he fears that he knows the truth: that he's really a creep, a weirdo, and doesn't belong.[4]

It doesn't matter how many people tell us we are special. A hole remains in us we can't fill. A fear about who we are haunts us, one that can't be assuaged: "If people really knew who I was, they would turn and walk away." Deep down, we know we are needy, we are anxious, we can't get things right.

Anxiety is debilitating at times. Angel once sat in front of a dear soul. The woman's legs bounced and her hands trembled. The echo

"Not enough" ran on a loop in her head. She had an abusive past that she kept secret. Shame, guilt, and fear were her only filters for processing.

Angel gets a front-row seat to the ways the Enemy seeks to destroy. This is the hard part of her job. "I just can't expose myself," the woman whispered over and over and over again, with hands over her face. Trauma does this. It speaks lies into our beings to the point of death.

This woman longed to have an impact on the lives of those she loved. She desperately wanted to experience intimacy in relationships. Yet she couldn't bear the thought of revealing who she was. She had learned at a young age that if you do enough, you can be enough. You can be free, loved, and forgiven . . . but only if you try hard enough.

She could only become by doing.

That was the lie that had destroyed her life. Angel's client had come to the end of herself in her fight to be good.

One of the great lies of the Enemy today is to claim truths about who we are in Christ without Christ as the foundation. To be clear, we cannot be what the Bible says we are without Christ. We cannot claim the truths of who we are in Christ if we do not first claim the truth of who we are *without* Christ.

And without Christ we are sinners, we are in rebellion against our Creator, and our hearts are ugly. We cannot be enough without Christ.

We cannot claim the truths of who we are in Christ if we do not first claim the truth of who we are *without* Christ.

However, our "before Christ" state shouldn't be overlooked, as discussed in the last chapter. We are all creations of the good Creator, and so we bear the marks of his care and craftsmanship. Because we are image bearers, we have a conscience that reflects the moral law of God. Our minds and our bodies reflect the careful design of God. Even without the transforming work of the Spirit of God in our lives, we still have a thirst for truth, an ability to love, and a desire to do good works. Of course, all of these are imperfect, but they are still in us.

And yet, we are not neutral spiritual beings. We are not the spiritual equivalent of Switzerland.

Most of us think we are primarily good. We might even think that picking up a book like this one is evidence of our innate goodness. We consider ourselves open-minded and even spiritual. We're just not religious. We're not extreme and a bit crazy like some of those really sold-out Christians we've met.

But do not be mistaken. Because of the fall, we are no longer naturally friends with God. We are foes. God has designed us for a specific relationship with himself and with others, but without purposefully choosing his terms, we reject his purpose. As much as we try, we can't hide behind our excuses: our discomfort with some of the things God has said; the frustration we have that God made only one way, Jesus, to come into relationship with himself; and the burdensome cost of a Christian life (reading the Bible, being part of a church, giving generously, serving).

If that sounds like you, then your beef is with your Creator, not Christians. And if the God of the universe really gave us a book where he disclosed the truth about himself, about you, and about the world, then you probably owe it to him (and yourself) to read it and come to terms with it. In that book, the Bible, God says that being cozy with the world is being an enemy of God (James 4:4). How cozy are you with the world? How much of your heart is absorbed with longing for more of what the world has to offer?

A recent survey revealed that the number one choice of career for teens is simply to be famous.[5] Another survey of millennials showed that they prioritized travel and owning a home over getting married or having children.[6] Of course, being single isn't a problem. In fact, the apostle Paul was single. But choosing the type of single life that is self-focused and doesn't strive to foster solid, reciprocal relationships isn't what God intended for us, single or not. What are your desires? If you were to be truly honest, what do you really want in life?

Our desires reveal our hearts. And our hearts do not naturally long for holiness above all things. Paul explains in Romans that Jesus died for us "while we were enemies" (Rom. 5:10). In his letter to the church at Philippi, Paul says that these "enemies of the cross of Christ" are those whose "god is their belly . . . with minds set on earthly things" (Phil. 3:18–19). The Puritan pastor Thomas Watson once said, "Sin not only makes us unlike God, but contrary to God."[7]

Light to Dark

But what our bellies desire always seems so good! The Bible has a powerful way of ironic understatement. When Eve is offered the forbidden fruit by the serpent, the serpent convinces her that God is actually withholding something good from her. The text says, "When the woman saw that the tree was good for food, and that it was a delight to the eyes, and that the tree was to be desired to make one wise, she took of its fruit and ate, and she also gave some to her husband who was with her, and he ate" (Gen. 3:6). Isn't this exactly how our sinful desires work? We convince ourselves that the object of our desire is delicious ("good for food"), beautiful ("a delight to the eyes") and will in fact be good for us ("was to be desired to make one wise").

Who is better at self-deceit than we are? And yet, how does every story of our fulfilling the desires of our bellies go? Each one ends the same way: disappointment, discouragement, and despair. The nineteenth-century pastor Thomas DeWitt Talmage once reflected, "Sin may open bright as the morning, but it will end dark as night."[8]

The world has been forever changed by the entrance of sin. We will have to fight against our inclinations if we want to experience God's best for us. Thomas Boston, a pastor in the seventeenth century, once said, "Sin has turned the world from a paradise into a thicket, there is no getting through without being scratched."[9]

Whatever desire you are trying to convince yourself will go well for you today is promised to have the same ending apart from life in Christ. Don't be deceived. If you continue on the path of self, you will receive the empty desires of your belly as a reward.

Powerless

In Ephesians 2:1–3, Paul gives us the bad news that this enemy state is not a situation we ourselves can change. We are powerless against it. He says:

> You were dead in the trespasses and sins in which you once walked, following the course of this world, following the prince of the power of the air, the spirit that is now at work in the sons of disobedience [that's us without Christ]— among whom we all once lived in the passions of our flesh, carrying out the desires of the body and the mind, and were by nature children of wrath, like the rest of mankind.

This is the human condition of all who are outside of Christ. It is our situation until we submit to God. In no uncertain terms, Paul tells us that "all have sinned and fall short of the glory of God" (Rom. 3:23).

You see, we prefer to justify ourselves by comparison. It's a lot easier to think of ourselves as being good when we use our neighbor as the yardstick of goodness. But who does the Bible say is the yardstick? God himself. How then do I answer the question about whether I am good? About whether I am a sinner? By stacking my heart up against God's.

That is sobering.

It's no surprise, then, that we are told,

> None is righteous, no, not one;
>> no one understands;
>> no one seeks for God.
> All have turned aside; together they have become worthless;
>> no one does good,
>> not even one. (Rom. 3:10–12)

This is not how we tend to think of sin. If we consider sin at all, we think of it as that which blocks us from the good life, the brokenness of the world that hinders us from enjoying our true self. We tend to frame the wrong in the world as that which hinders us from being our true selves, and our true selves are the selves we think we can uncover if we are just able to slip away from the anxieties of the modern world. "If I could just get away," we think. "If I could just not have these pressures, then I could be my best self." But our best self is never found when we remove the pressures and feed our appetites.

Adam Sandler had a bit on *Saturday Night Live* where he plays a character named Joe Romano, an Italian tour guide very concerned about making sure the expectations of his potential clients aren't too high. In the parody commercial, Romano reminds his customers, "If you're sad now, you might still feel sad there. . . . You're still going to be you on vacation."[10] It's so true.

We tell ourselves that if only we could experience life without our current stress, or without the difficult people in our lives, or without the pain we are experiencing, or without our financial hardships, *then* we would be able to experience our true, best selves. But the reality is sobering.

When the financial hardship is lifted, we become greedier; when the physical pain dissipates, our spiritual lives shrivel up; when we go on vacation, we become even more irritable. Fixing our circumstances doesn't fix the ache. How can that be?

Because our ultimate issue is with ourselves, not with what's out there. Because when we're freed to realize our best selves, what we discover isn't our best selves but very broken selves.

This is a biblical truth. We can get everything we want, and we will still be sad. Because we are sinful. This tragic state is no small matter.

The Weight of Sin

If you read the Bible, you'll realize something pretty quickly. God doesn't treat sin lightly. Adam and Eve eat a piece of fruit they aren't supposed to, and they are banished from the garden of Eden and the presence of God. Sin has consequences.

When I was young, I was a master at the speed apology. I would cheat at a game or take something that was my sister's, then quickly feel remorseful and apologize before my sister could even react. My apology would escalate the situation because I wasn't honestly owning my offense. Rather, I was trying to move past my offense. I slapped the "I'm-sorry" Band-Aid on anything I did to hurt my relationship with my sister. I thought I could restore our relationship too easily.

But reversing sin isn't that easy. After the garden of Eden and before the arrival of Jesus, God set up an entire system with his covenant people in which they had to offer animals as sacrifices to atone for their sin before this holy Being. The entire book of Leviticus is about this system. Much of the book of Deuteronomy emphasizes how important following this system is. The books of the Law and Prophets remind us how holy God is and of the need to atone for sin to enter God's presence. But it turns out that even this elaborate system isn't enough to atone for our sins, and so God offers his own Son as the only perfect sacrifice to make things right between us and God (see Heb. 9).

Do you consider that even your smallest indiscretions separate you from God? We're not talking the red-letter sins that you think you steer clear of, such as theft, adultery, and murder. We're talking run-of-the-mill sin that mars each of our days. The white lies you tell your boss. The anger that flares in your heart when you're cut off while driving. The porn you dabble with. We can't be reconciled to God with even this pollution in our hearts.

God offers his own Son as the only perfect sacrifice to make things right between us and God.

It reveals not how curmudgeonly or antiquated the God of the Bible is that this sin separates us from him but rather how small our understanding is of his purity, perfection, and holiness.

We try to pull ourselves up by our psychological bootstraps and convince ourselves that we are great just as we are. We look in the mirror and repeat Stuart Smalley's immortal words: "I'm good enough, I'm smart enough, and doggone it, people like me."[11] And yet, the hollow ring of those words only creates an ache, considering the pain, loss, and questions that echo in our hearts. There aren't enough coffee mugs, T-shirts, and tattoos in the world to mask the shadow that darkens our hearts: I'm not enough, and I know my heart is anything but beautiful.

Tim and Kathy Keller captured the gospel message this way: "We are more sinful and flawed in ourselves than we ever dared believe, yet at the very same time we are more loved and accepted in Jesus Christ than we ever dared hope."[12] We are sinners who can't make ourselves right. We must start there. We must start with open hands and needy hearts.

God invites you to come as you are: raw, vulnerable, transparent, and needy. This is the honest self: "God, as much as I know how to do, I confess my desperation to you. I need your Spirit to come alive in me. Right now. You know what I need. Mold me. Shape me. Nothing in me is good unless your Spirit intersects with it and you have your way." We have to look to the One who created us and trust him. There's no other hope.

But there is good news: Our Creator has sent his Son for us to make right what we have made wrong, to transform our identity from enemy to child, from purposeless to purposeful, from sinner to saint, from slave to free. Our weakness is strength because of who we are in him (2 Cor. 12:9–10). Augustine once noted, "He that is good is free, though he be a slave; he that is evil is a slave, though he be a king."[13]

Made Good

Our hearts are deceitful. They insist we can be enough if we do enough and become enough on our own.

That thirst for righteousness is God-given. God has made us to reflect his goodness. He has made us for good works (Eph. 2:10). And he has made us for purity.

God invites us to take the posture of humility and to recognize our neediness. Our need can be a gift if we allow it to shift our dependence from self to the Creator. Jesus says we don't have to be enough: he is enough for us.

Can you taste the freedom? Can you taste the peace? Can you taste the rest? The burden is no longer yours to bear in the fight to be good. If Jesus is my master, and he says I am needy, then I am allowed to be needy and to acknowledge that need to him. When we live in Christ's provision of goodness, we feel no shame when we ask for help. Jesus refers to this as being "poor in spirit" (Matt. 5:3).

His Spirit is living. The Holy Spirit is active and has the power to move in you. You don't need to know what that looks like; you just need to make yourself available to the Spirit's work.

It is only when we turn away from the pursuit of being good in our own strength that we can experience the true goodness of Christ. Our Creator gave us our hunger for righteousness, and he can satisfy it through Jesus. Jesus is righteous and gives us his righteousness. Imagine yourself at the base of the cross, humbly bowing below Christ's feet. His blood drips onto you, and you are purified. It is a spiritual infusion of his crimson blood making you white as snow (Isa. 1:18).

We are made to be good. We just cannot make ourselves good.

PRAYER

Creator, forgive me for my rebellion against you. I have considered my natural inclinations good when they have been evil. I have trusted myself when I am untrustworthy. I have rejected you as my Creator and have chosen myself time and time again. I've thought that if I just tried harder or were smarter, I might be able to dig myself out of the holes I've dug. I confess that my only hope is in you. Please help me find my identity in who you say I am. Amen.

Independence
Finding Freedom as a Servant

⁓

I am no bird; and no net ensnares me; I am a free human being with an independent will.
—Charlotte Brontë, *Jane Eyre*

Live as people who are free, not using your freedom as a cover-up for evil, but living as servants of God.
—Peter

The greatest among you shall be your servant.
—Jesus

The only freedom that man ever has is when he becomes a slave to Jesus Christ.
—R. C. Sproul

TRADING FACES

ANGEL

"GOD GAVE US ALCOHOL AND women, and I enjoy both. I'm not sinning. My conscience is clear." Jordan was clearly miffed. John had asked him, one of our ministry leaders, to reconsider his social media posts that highlighted a beach trip replete with alcohol, nightclubs, and young ladies draped on him.

✏

The world echoes our corrupt hearts: "Take what you want, how you want it, when you want it."

John and I were three years into full-time ministry when it felt as though the cage of ministry responsibilities was closing in on us. We were suffocating. Each of us had escalating responsibilities either at church or in the counseling office, and those responsibilities chipped away at our freedom. Then, while we were already stretched thin, tragedy struck. A staff member attempted suicide, and the resultant care for him and the congregation stretched John to the breaking point. Meanwhile, a sexual sin by my boss took me past the breaking point.

I was furious—with God most of all. *This is not what I signed up for*, I thought. *This is not what ministry is supposed to be. What kind of God takes your sacrifice of ministry and then demands more of you? What kind of God is so cruel that he squeezes you for all you're worth and then demands one more thing?*

This was no God I was willing to serve. I had signed up to serve a loving, merciful, and kind God, not a vengeful, hateful, imprisoning God.

So I rejected him. I wouldn't serve him. I would serve myself, explore the independence I deserved.

I ran to the gym, trying to find a new identity there. I ran to multiple new careers—photography and working at Lululemon Ath-letica among them. I became a hardcore yoga junkie. Ultimately, I chose to go down a path that led me to reject John and find love in the arms of other men.[1]

Had I found freedom? No. I was shackled to sin. It would take years and God's miraculous hand to rescue me from the bondage I put myself in.

So what is freedom, and where do we find it?

"I Could Be Literally Anything"

Recently we were listening to a podcast with an influential leader. She gushed about her mom: "When I was little, she never stopped telling me I could be literally anything." There is something beau-tiful in that encouragement. And her statement contains a seed of truth. For many of us, our identities formed with this sense of un-bounded possibility. There was nothing we couldn't do if we put our minds to it.

And yet, almost anyone outside of a late twentieth- and early twenty-first-century Western context would find this sort of un-bridled encouragement completely befuddling. The idea of having boundless vocational options—or any options, for that matter—is a peculiarly modern and Western notion.

We are told that we are defined by our independence. If we have a birthright as Americans, it is our freedom. We are told it is the most important commodity we possess. We are free to do what we want, be what we want, love who we want.

We celebrate those who have made themselves something out of nothing. Consider the following three celebrity stories, which we ap-plaud as a culture.

Michael Jordan's story always begins with him getting cut from his high school basketball team. In its telling and retelling, it's a story of overcoming the odds and the doubters and ending with perhaps the greatest basketball player to live. Jordan even shared this story in his Hall of Fame acceptance speech. It's interesting to note, however, that in the story Jordan's coach has shared publicly, Jordan wasn't actually cut. He just played JV instead of varsity during his sophomore year.[2]

We are told that we are free to do what we want, be what we want, love who we want.

Then there's Stefani Joanne Angelina Germanotta's story. Stefani's story begins with her being told that she was too ugly and not talented enough to make it in music or theater. In her telling, she was discovered in a burlesque show. From these humble beginnings, this Yonkers-born girl catapulted to mega pop stardom as Lady Gaga. Digging deeper, however, we learn that she was accepted into Juilliard at age eleven and then received a prestigious early admission to NYU's Tisch School of the Arts.[3]

What about J. K. Rowling? The story goes that she had just gone through a divorce and was living on government aid, and her book about a wizard named Harry Potter had been rejected dozens of times before she became the best-selling contemporary fiction author. But the broader reality includes Rowling's privileged childhood, excellent education, and the fact that she had been writing books since age six.[4]

These tales of gutsy rags-to-riches success are like those we learn from childhood, stories told to us by our grandparents, parents, and teachers. We have a thirst for independence, self-actualization, being discovered as the diamond in the rough. We chafe at the strictures most have lived under, environments that severely limited freedom and opportunities.

We don't want to be hemmed in or controlled. The idea of growing up as most in the history of the world have—with a predetermined vocation and spouse—makes us scoff. No one could possibly live like that.

Our hearts tell us we will be happy if we have more options, but radical freedom actually has the opposite effect. Surprisingly, psychological research tells us that increased choice diminishes our happiness.[5] A child without a bedtime, nutritional guardrails, or discipline is not only ill behaved but anxious and unhappy.

Spirituality Is Our Sacred Space

In the modern West, our freedom extends beyond our ability to choose our vocation and spouse. We have the freedom to create our own spirituality. We believe that the spiritual world is a private world, a place we can craft to our own liking. The sacred is personal. The personal is sacred.

The notion that our spirituality is located in a private place between us and our experience of the divine is a relatively new idea. It is also a rare point of agreement between those who are ideologically on opposite sides of the spectrum. It seems we all can agree that no one should dictate another person's religious beliefs.

For some, the true north on their compass is their conception of love. For the other side, the true north is their conception of truth. But for both, their spiritual lives are their own. It's no surprise that church attendance has so dramatically dipped in the past decade.[6] For everything we in the West fight over, we appear to agree on one thing: no institution will define our spirituality. Our spiritual life is ours, and whatever beliefs we craft in that deeply personal space are unimpeachable.

We think we are creating a meaningful path. Yet many have a haunting sense that they are lost in these spiritual woods. If our compass comes from within, how do we know it is directing us somewhere that actually exists? Where is our destination? And how do we know we will get there?

Star of the Show

There are a lot of conversations today about building your platform and your brand. Many claim the job title of "influencer" or "social media influencer." There is something attractive about wielding influence. "What could I do with fame?" we ponder. "What impact could I have?"

You can pour your energy into building your own kingdom. But what will last of it? Who will remember you? What are you living for?

When John was in college on the North Shore of Massachusetts, the movie *The Perfect Storm* was being filmed in the area. Starring George Clooney and Mark Wahlberg, it was based on the true story of a commercial fishing boat that was lost at sea. The movie was filmed in Gloucester, Massachusetts, where the boat departed for its fateful voyage.

A handful of John's friends spent weeks waiting in line for the opportunity to be extras in the movie. Sure enough, when the movie aired, a couple of them had a second or two of anonymous fame. The friends watched the movie together and waited for their big moment. "There I am!" they pointed as their faces flashed on the screen. They paused the movie to make the moment last just a little longer.

We all want to be part of something bigger. It's how our big Creator has made us. We long to be part of something meaningful. Yet if we're honest, we don't want to be merely an extra; we want to be the lead. How many of us live lives where we are the star of our own reality show that will never air?

When John was a kid, he imagined there were scouts from the local University of Arizona basketball team who were videotaping and watching him practice alone at his neighborhood court. When he hit that fade-away jump shot from the corner that he had been working on forever, he tried to act nonchalant so they would be impressed with his lack of excitement.

Most of us live our lives longing for our five minutes of fame (how about seven for me, God?), yearning to be discovered, hoping our YouTube video goes viral. In our heart of hearts, many of us want the world to revolve around us. We want our lives to be on a bigger stage. It's why there is a business of selling followers on social media. We want a bigger audience, even if it's an audience of fake people. A 2017 survey showed that millennials value fame highly. Thirty percent would prefer to be famous rather than to be a lawyer; 23 percent would choose fame over being a doctor; and 8 percent would cut off ties to their family in exchange for fame.[7]

In our heart of hearts, many of us want the world to revolve around us.

How foolish of us! Can you tell me the names of any of your great-great-grandparents? Can you tell me one thing they did in their lives? Friend, from a human perspective, we will all be forgotten. Poet Henry Austin Dobson once wrote, "Fame is a food that dead men eat."[8]

The irony is that when we pursue our own glory and platform, we are living in true enslavement. The apostle Paul wrote, "If we have been united with him [Jesus] in a death like his, we shall certainly be united with him in a resurrection like his. We know that our old self was crucified with him in order that the body of sin might be brought to nothing, so that we would no longer be *enslaved to sin*" (Rom. 6:5–6, my emphasis).

Sin—grappling for self—is a cruel master. There is never enough fame, glory, money, love, respect, sexual gratification. "Am I now seeking the approval of man, or of God? Or am I trying to please man? If I were still trying to please man, I would not be a servant of Christ" (Gal. 1:10). Our flesh demands more and more. It is not only hard drugs that have diminishing returns. It is anything of the flesh. And so, even as we seek more, we find ourselves with less.

Freedom to Serve

God has not given us self-actualizing independence. He did not intend for us to twist the freedom he gives us for his purposes into freedom to be used for our own agendas. To use our freedom for our personal gain is to buy into the lie of the Enemy.

Surprising to our Western sensibilities, the Bible unflinchingly refers to Christians not as individualists but as servants or slaves (in Greek the word is *duolos*, which can be translated as either servant or slave, depending on the context[9]). Servants are those who choose to serve another. Slaves are those who must serve someone else because they are owned by that person. In Christ, both senses are true for the Christian. Because Christ has paid our ransom, we can joyfully be his slave *and* choose to serve him.

Our Western individuality is undone when we see ourselves as servants. Servants seek the fulfillment of their masters before they seek fulfilling themselves. This hardly fits with our American notions of what our lives are supposed to look like. It's not surprising, then, that more than a few pastors and churches have erased the biblical call on us to be servants of Christ. Unfortunately, doing so causes us to miss out on freeing truths about who we are.

Peter's perspective is profound: we are free in Christ, and yet that freedom is to be used for our Master. Peter says, "Live as people who are free, not using your freedom as a cover-up for evil, but living as servants of God" (1 Peter 2:16).

We are tempted to believe that freedom is found when we achieve self-mastery. But true freedom is only found when Christ is our Master. The freedom our flesh and the world offers is no freedom at all, but bondage. To be a slave to Christ is to experience true freedom. How can that be? Because to be Jesus's servant is to live as our Creator intended us to live. It is to be an agent of the One who lived the perfect human life. When we look at Jesus, we see a life we long to emulate, and his life was the life of a servant. Just as Jesus cared for the poor, weak, and needy, we are purposed as God's servants to selflessly love neighbors, children, widows, and orphans.

True freedom is only found when Christ is our Master.

It's important to stop here and address our terms. Our tendency is to transpose the despicable history of slavery in our country onto the biblical idea of servanthood. That has the possibility of doing harm to our understanding of the character of God and the nature of servanthood. God set up clear boundaries in the law to protect Israelite slaves. In Leviticus 25, for instance, God mandates that the non-Israelite master "shall treat [the slave] as a worker hired year by year. He shall not rule ruthlessly over him in your sight. And if he is not redeemed by these means, then he and his children with him shall be released in the year of jubilee. For it is to me that the people of Israel are servants. They are my servants whom I brought out of the land of Egypt: I am the LORD your God" (vv. 53–55).

Many understandably shudder at using the language of slavery for our relationship with God when viewed against the backdrop of the horrors of antebellum American slavery. But that isn't our relationship with God. He is never the master with whip in hand, mistreating slaves he holds against their will. God's heart toward us is for our good. He is a good and perfect master.

But he is still our Lord.

So what does it look like for God to be our Lord and for us to be his willing servants? Let your imagination transport you to a Palestinian home in the sixth century BC. Your vocation as a farmer was determined by your father. Your wife is your vocational partner.

She tends the fields and cares for the livestock with you. You are a farmer because your father was a farmer. Your cousin is a shepherd, as his father was. If your father was a mason, you would work in construction. If your father was a government official, that would be your path.

In this world, the role of a servant was a legitimate occupation. The role of a servant would have been similar to a nanny or housekeeper or groundskeeper. Biblical law spills quite a bit of ink protecting the slave as a member of the family.[10]

It was not uncommon, in fact, for someone who fell upon hard times to sell himself to someone else to serve as a slave. Doing so might even mean the promise of a better life—of a home with meals provided.

While some became servants in order to pay off debt, even that arrangement was protected. Masters were not to create situations in which slaves couldn't work off their debts. As a double protection, every fiftieth year was a Jubilee for all of Israel, when every servant was freed. It is unclear whether Israel faithfully followed this practice as God prescribed, but the fact that God ordained it shows the ethic he intended.

One might expect that when servants achieved their financial freedom, they would immediately leave their master's home. But that was not necessarily so. The conditions for some servants was good enough that, according to Jewish law, they could choose to stay in their master's home permanently. There was even a ceremony in which the servant would have their earlobe pierced with an awl, marking them as a permanent servant of their master and a member of the household. This special, lifelong bond between master and servant was freely chosen by the servant. Whenever you saw a slave with a pierced lobe, you realized this was someone serving their master out of gratitude and affection, not compulsion.

It's this kind of relationship God desires. And he has every right to be our master. Why? Broadly, the answer is that he is God. He is *the* Sovereign. Unlike us, he is truly independent. He is the source of all life. All good things flow from him. He holds the cosmos in the palm of his hand, and not a single quark wanders outside his control. More personally, he has the right to be *your* master because he created you and then he paid the ransom for your salvation. He purchased you with a price: his own blood.

The apostle Thomas understood this when he responded to the resurrected Jesus, "My Lord and my God!" (John 20:28). Thomas struggled to believe that Jesus could have been resurrected from the dead. But when he came face-to-face with the resurrected Jesus, he knew it wasn't mere belief that Jesus required of him—it was submission. Jesus was no mere rabbi. He held the keys to life and death.

This is no con. When you trust in Christ, you don't just trust him to save you. You trust him as your new master, and you choose to serve and obey him. This means that we submit to his commandments, even when they aren't comfortable or don't make sense to us.

Christ the Servant

We can almost hear your Western ideology rebelling at the thought of being a servant. But hold up. It isn't a lowly position. Let's not forget that God understands what it is to be a servant, and not just conceptually. He understands it personally. In Philippians 2:7, Paul reminds us that Christ "emptied himself, by taking the form of a servant."

Jesus's servant-heartedness did not end at his becoming human. Jesus lived a life of service. On his final day, he knelt before his disciples with a towel wrapped around his waist and served them as only the lowest servants did: by washing his disciples' sweaty, smelly, and dusty feet. And then he urged them to follow his example: "If I then, your Lord and Teacher, have washed your feet, you also ought to wash one another's feet. For I have given you an example, that you also should do just as I have done to you. Truly, truly, I say to you, a servant is not greater than his master, nor is a messenger greater than the one who sent him. If you know these things, blessed are you if you do them" (John 13:14–17). Jesus became a servant so that you might be his servant.

If the God of the universe willingly knelt to wash the feet of his people, it's more than fair for him to ask us to do the same, is it not?

The shape of our service is Christ. "The Lord's servant must not be quarrelsome but kind to everyone, able to teach, patiently enduring evil" (2 Tim. 2:24). How much evil have you endured as Christ's servant? How often have you bitten your tongue when baited?

Our hearts naturally want to exert themselves, to show others that we're right, to correct wrongs done against us. But there is Jesus, at the feet of those he poured years into and who will abandon him in but a few hours. He kneels, wiping the feet of those who will be responsible for a nail being driven into his own feet a day later. Our Savior is indeed the form of a servant, and he calls us to die to our egos, die to our pride, and serve with joy.

Doorkeepers

Jesus's sacrifice and his invitation for us to sacrifice are aimed at bringing about the grandest enterprise in the history of the universe: the kingdom of God. Scripture tells us that God's kingdom is where he breaks through the injustice, anxiety, and pain of this world and ushers in his goodness, love, and peace. The kingdom of God began breaking in when Jesus came to the world in flesh as the God-man, and it continues to advance through the work of the Holy Spirit through God's people. The great irony is that God is capable of ushering in his kingdom all on his own, yet he chooses to allow you and me to participate so we can find freedom from life's hurts! God's kingdom is what we were made for and is glorious beyond our wildest imagination.

When we see the aim of servanthood—our good—we value the gift of it. Consider the sons of Korah, who served in the tabernacle. They knew there was nothing that compared with being in the presence of God. All else paled in comparison to being face-to-face with the great I Am. Just a taste of God's presence stirred one's heart like nothing else:

> My soul longs, yes, faints
> > for the courts of the LORD;
> my heart and flesh sing for joy
> > to the living God. (Ps. 84:2)

The sons of Korah say that serving in the lowest station at the very edges of the presence of God far surpasses being a master in one's own tent. They sing:

> A day in your courts is better
> > than a thousand elsewhere.
> I would rather be a doorkeeper in the house of my God
> > than dwell in the tents of wickedness. (v. 10)

Have you experienced the power and presence of God such that it has shaped your longings in this way? Do you know the heart of your Master? Do you know his voice? Do you know his embrace? On this earth we experience but the most fleeting whisper of God's voice, the gentlest touch of his hand. Can you imagine his clear, warm, and loving voice speaking to you? Can you imagine his strong and tender embrace enveloping you?

Jesus shares a story of servants who are given gifts by their master. Jesus paints the picture of the day we will all meet our Master face-to-face. On that day God will look into your eyes and speak this profound blessing over you: "Well done, good and faithful servant"

(Matt. 25:23). The anxieties and sorrows of the world will be gone, and the joy and peace of your Savior will envelop you.

Building God's House

In her book *Grit*, Angela Duckworth tells the story of three apocryphal medieval bricklayers. Each has a very different perspective on their task. "Three bricklayers are asked, 'What are you doing?' The first says, 'I am laying bricks.' The second says, 'I am building a church.' And the third says, 'I am building the house of God.' The first bricklayer has a job. The second has a career. The third has a calling."[11]

Are you able to raise your eyes off of your bricks? Can you see what God is using your service for? Do you understand your calling as a servant of the Most High? Do you understand your role in the most incredible story ever written?

In John's Gospel, he explains that there were those in positions of power who believed in Jesus, but they couldn't bear to give up the acceptance of the public. They weren't willing to part with their tiny little sliver of the stage for the sake of Jesus. John says, "They loved the glory that comes from man more than the glory that comes from God" (John 12:43).

Do you understand your calling as a servant of the Most High in the most incredible story ever written?

On the flip side, Jesus tells a parable of a beggar who laid at the gate of a man who had all the glory the world could offer. The beggar, Lazarus, knew God and was carried off by angels at his death to share a table with Abraham. But the rich man, after dying, suffered in torment.

In Matthew 23:11 Jesus says, "The greatest among you shall be your servant." Jesus paints a picture of our final day, face-to-face with God, in the company of those who have lived lives poured out for his glory. Do you want to be great in the eyes of Jesus? Be a servant.

When God foretold the miraculous moment when he would give his people the Holy Spirit, he said, "Even on the male and female servants in those days I will pour out my Spirit" (Joel 2:29). We are servants filled with the Spirit.

Ironically, when we embrace our identity as a lowly servant, we join a litany of great saints whose names are remembered.

John calls Moses "the servant of God" (Rev. 15:3). Mary responds to the angel Gabriel by saying, "I am the servant of the Lord" (Luke 1:38).

Paul refers to himself as a servant on many occasions (Rom. 1:1; 1 Cor. 3:5; Phil. 1:1; Titus 1:1) and states that he is "a servant to all, that I might win more of them [for Christ]" (1 Cor. 9:19). "What we proclaim is not ourselves," he tells the Corinthian believers, "but Jesus Christ as Lord, with ourselves as your servants for Jesus' sake" (2 Cor. 4:5). It is because of his lowly service that he can be trusted, Paul says: "As servants of God we commend ourselves in every way: by great endurance, in afflictions, hardships, calamities," and many more hallmarks of his humble, others-focused character (2 Cor. 6:4–10). And he is in good company. Paul refers to many others as servants as well, including Phoebe (Rom. 16:1), Apollos (1 Cor. 3:5), Epaphras (Col. 1:7), Tychicus (Col. 4:7), and Timothy (Phil. 1:1).

James begins his letter with this introduction: "James, a servant of God and of the Lord Jesus Christ" (James 1:1). Jude begins his letter in similar fashion: "Jude, a servant of Jesus Christ and brother of James" (Jude v. 1). And John likewise begins his revelation to the seven churches by referring to himself and his fellow brothers and sisters in Christ as servants.

What a glory to be called a servant of the Most High! What a privilege to serve the most glorious Being, the greatest hero on history's stage, and to know that our service is noticed and praised by him. And that our service helps advance his great purposes.

As servants, we are invited in every encounter with another person to see them as image bearers of the Creator. They are those who, like you, desire to love and be loved. As I talk with those who are introverts, those who hide in public, and those who perceive themselves as socially awkward, I always find it a fun conversation to invite them into a scene where they give themselves permission to take their focus off their own discomfort and look at the person in front of them as one whom the Creator breathed his breath into. Each person is made to be loved and seen and known. Servants set aside their desire for comfort for the sake of honoring their master.

As servants, we are invited in every encounter with another person to see them as image bearers of the Creator.

When we are God's servants, our focus is on pleasing him and caring for those around us. We care less about ourselves and more about those he's called us to serve. Everyone in front of us has a story. Many desperately want to be seen. Living as a servant might mean something as simple as addressing the cashier by name and smiling. It might mean asking a question that engages them to share a story about their day. As servants we care for others' emotional and spiritual needs.

This also ought to reshape the way that we understand our vocations on this earth. In Colossians 3:23–24 Paul encourages Christian servants that their work was their calling! No matter our vocation, whether a president or a dishwasher, we are all servants of God. There is no platform so big on earth that is not dwarfed by this great honor. And there is no vocation so unseen that the hosts of heaven do not look on, cheering faithful obedience done to the praise of God's grace.

Our flesh longs for independence. However, what we think is freedom is enslavement. True freedom comes from our benevolent Master, who welcomes us as his servants. We experience true freedom as we step into the joy of serving him. Nothing could be more ennobling and gratifying than doing the work of our glorious Lord.

PRAYER

Master, forgive me for my stubborn independence. Forgive me for in so many ways acting like I am my own master. What utter foolishness! What bullheadedness! What arrogance. Forgive me. It is my delight to serve you. Please give me a heart of service. Give me, like Jesus at the Last Supper, eyes to see those who can be served. Teach me to put myself at the lowest place so that others might be lifted up around me. Give me pleasure as I serve for the honor of your great name, most high Master. Amen.

Individuality
Finding Rest as a Sheep of the Good Shepherd

⌒

Better one day as a lion than a hundred years as a sheep.
—Benito Mussolini

Normal is not something to aspire to,
it's something to get away from.
—Jodie Foster

When we face death, we have the same choice before us as
we have in every area of life: Who will be our shepherd?
—David Powlison

ANGEL

"YOU'RE GOING TO HAVE TO get used to my being blunt," a coworker shared with John after he had just leveled some criticism at the church. "I'm an ENTJ—a commander. Take me or leave me." He said it with a grin, but he was serious. He was giving John a gentle warning that he was different from other employees. If he had feedback to offer, he was going to let John have it.

⌇

There is no shortage of these types of tests. From discovering what fruit, animal, or *The Office* character you are, to more serious explorations of personality such as StrengthsFinder, Enneagram, Myers-Briggs, and DiSC, there are many avenues to discern how you interpret and understand yourself. For many, understanding themselves through their personality types provides insight into how God has made them. Such tests can help you understand your wiring and where God might be calling you vocationally. They help you understand the wonderful aspects of your personality as well as the difficult aspects. They help you grow in self-awareness and in appreciation of others. They make teams stronger and help you understand what unique contributions you might be able to make.

The two tests John and I appreciate most are CliftonStrengths (formerly StrengthsFinder) and Enneagram.[1] CliftonStrengths "explains how you are uniquely powerful," defining "the ways you most naturally think, feel and behave."[2] We have found CliftonStrengths to be particularly helpful in professional environments. It offers excellent insight into what your optimal contribution to a team might be and in what areas you should lean on your coworkers for the strengths they contribute. The fundamental premise of CliftonStrengths is that we are at our best when operating in the areas where we are most gifted. CliftonStrengths challenges businesses that expend their best energy fixing employees' weaknesses rather than deploying employees in their areas of strength. On a personal level, the creators of CliftonStrengths insist that too often we try to fix our weaknesses instead of leaning into our strengths. We agree.

The Enneagram is a typology of nine personality types that aids in self-awareness, self-understanding, and self-development. It can be helpful for spiritual growth when used to recognize spiritual struggles and weaknesses. When explored in a Christian context, each of the Enneagram types has certain associated sin tendencies. Every individual struggles with particular temptations more than others. One might have a particular battle with lust, while another might fight hard against sloth, and someone else might find that greed can be their downfall. Considering your area of spiritual vulnerability provides the opportunity to grow in spiritual awareness and sanctification.

Considering your area of spiritual vulnerability provides the opportunity to grow in spiritual awareness and sanctification.

Ian Morgan Cron, coauthor with Suzanne Stabile of a book on the Enneagram, *The Road Back to You*, says, "Buried in the deepest precincts of being I sense there's a truer, more luminous expression of myself, and that as long as I remain estranged from it I will never feel fully alive or whole. Maybe you have felt the same."[3] The hope of a "more luminous expression" of ourselves is a grand promise, one that Cron asserts the Enneagram can fulfill.

John and I disagree. As a gift for enhancing self-awareness, "typing" is good, but personality types are not the truest, most "luminous expression" of a person. Yes, even personalities are substitute identities for who God made each of us to be. When you ask, "Who am I?" your personality is a secondary, not primary, answer to that question. There are dangers when we reduce ourselves to our personality type. Ironically, we can both overstate our individuality (forgetting we are all the sheep of God's pasture) and understate it (humanity cannot be reduced to any number of "types"). We can also give ourselves license to not grow. A *New Yorker* cartoon pointedly demonstrates this. In it, one man shares with a friend, "Now that I know my personality type, I have an excuse for behaving exactly the same."[4]

First, You Are the Same

It's good to understand your particular personality and giftings. But what if the answer to "Who am I?" is not found in a personality test but rather in God's Word? What if the deepest truth about who you are is something you share with others, not something that differentiates you?

What if exploring what makes us the same is what truly makes us special?

Author Frederick Buechner once commented, "The original, shimmering self gets buried so deep that most of us end up hardly living out of it at all. Instead we live out all the other selves, which we are constantly putting on and taking off like coats and hats against the world's weather."[5] Buechner is right. But our "original, shimmering self" is not found on an individual journey of personality type; it is found on a shared biblical journey.

The first two humans, Adam and Eve, demonstrate this profound "sameness." Despite their different genders, at their core they had the same identity. The first two descriptions of us in the Bible reveal how similar we are. As God brings his creation to a close, he says, "Let us make man in our image, after our likeness" (Gen. 1:26). And then God does just that. The text makes it clear that it is not just Adam but Eve, too, who is made in God's image:

> So God created man in his own image,
>   in the image of God he created him;
>   male and female he created them. (v. 27)

The first description is that we, male and female, are the same: made in God's image. The second description is like the first. In

Genesis 2, we get a more detailed description of how God made Adam and Eve, and we learn that God formed Eve out of Adam's rib. When Adam sees Eve for the first time, his jaw doesn't drop at how different she is from himself—he marvels at how similar she is:

> This at last is bone of my bones
>> and flesh of my flesh;
> she shall be called Woman,
>> because she was taken out of Man. (v. 23)

While Genesis 1 and 2 emphasize our shared humanity and the fact that we bear our Creator's image, our modern obsession is with highlighting our differences. Where God finds our primary value in what we share (reflecting his image), we find our primary value in what makes us unique.

To be clear, the point here isn't that there are not God-ordained gender differences (there are), or that we don't have unique personalities (we do); rather, the point is that our identity is grounded first in what we share, not in what separates us.

Busyness and Rest

Our obsession with personalities, and with finding our identities in them, perpetuates one of our cultural sicknesses: we have replaced a call to *be* with a call to *do*. When our identity is defined by what we produce, anxiety will always follow. The fear of not *doing* enough *is* the fear of not *being* enough. The shadow of who we are in a personality-focused world is fear.

Whatever personality test you use to help define your personality, one of the core questions being asked is, "How do you engage with the world?" For instance, the StrengthsFinder test reveals where you may best contribute to your team. Do you have a unique ability to adapt to your situation, an unusual capacity to focus, a voracious appetite for learning, a catalog of details filed in your brain, a deep empathy for people, or an ability to powerfully persuade? Enneagram helps us consider the way we understand the world and navigate our emotions. Do you see the world as a challenge to be defeated? Or a problem to be solved? Or a party to be enjoyed?

We can't say it enough: Those are valuable things to learn about yourself, but they are not your ultimate identity. If personality is your bedrock identity, your tendency may be to exhaust yourself as you try to optimize yourself. What if your true and deeper identity brings rest rather than exhaustion?

> **If personality is your bedrock identity, you may exhaust yourself as you try to optimize yourself.**

Indeed, ours is an age of exhaustion. "No rest for the weary" is our de facto motto.

Most of us have a love-hate relationship with the twins of anxiety and exhaustion. Many of us can hardly imagine ourselves free from their clutches. I once asked a client, "What does rest look like for you?" She paused and answered, "Rest is guilt. If you are not doing something, you are lazy. If you are lazy, you are a worthless person. As a kid, I learned that watching TV is slothful. I had to earn that privilege. As an adult, my rule is that I have to be eating while watching my Netflix show so that I'm using the time efficiently. I can't binge-watch something because then I would be a bum. I even tried once to stay in my pj's all day, and I got so antsy by noon, I had to work out and change. I don't know how to rest. Rest is wasteful. I like feeling productive. If I am not accomplishing something, I am a waste of a person." This woman could not rest because she did not know who she was if she was not producing something. To rest was antithetical to who she thought she was.

We have a hyperproductive friend who often repeated the common quote, "I'll sleep when I'm dead." In a world where the setting sun does nothing to inhibit our productivity, we are more apt than ever to be caught up in this hamster wheel. (Ironically, I am typing this sentence at 10:50 p.m. "Physician, heal thyself!")

We get a kick out of the episode of the classic television show *Seinfeld* where Kramer decides he needs to maximize his productivity, so he incorporates the polyphasic method: in place of a night's sleep, you substitute twenty-minute naps every three hours around the clock. Unsurprisingly, the results are hilarious and disastrous.

What if you could experience rest? Would you be willing to rest? Would you be willing to try to find yourself apart from what you do?

We Need the Shepherd

We cannot find rest on our own terms. We can only find it in the presence of the Good Shepherd, who knows us and calls us to *his* rest.

At some point during David's long days protecting his flock, God revealed to David that he was David's shepherd. Psalm 23 is a reflection on the truth that God is our shepherd, and we are his sheep. You will be tempted to jump over the psalm because you know it. But slow down and read the psalm like it's your first time reading it.

The LORD is my shepherd; I shall not want.
　He makes me lie down in green pastures.
He leads me beside still waters.
　He restores my soul.
He leads me in paths of righteousness for his name's sake.

Even though I walk through the valley of the shadow of death,
　I will fear no evil,
for you are with me;
　　your rod and your staff,
　　they comfort me.

You prepare a table before me
    in the presence of my enemies;
you anoint my head with oil;
    my cup overflows.
Surely goodness and mercy shall follow me
    all the days of my life,
and I shall dwell in the house of the LORD forever.

Would you read that again? This time pause, reflect, and listen to the Shepherd's voice. Imagine the setting—the green grass, the water reflecting the trees, a picnic, the whole setup. What has he prepared for you?

In order to find what he offers, we have to release our attempts to save ourselves through molding our personality and accept who he says we are. Who does he say you are? You are his sheep.

Culturally, we use the word *sheep* as a pejorative: "Don't be such a sheep!" Supposedly, Mussolini once said, "Better one day as a lion than a hundred years as a sheep."[6] This sounds like it was written in America circa 2022. Why do we denigrate sheep? Because they are all the same. They do the same stuff. They eat, they sleep, they follow. And they are not smart. We think similarity and simpleness are flaws. We think our unique attributes and intelligence are what make us important. But what really sets us apart is that we are individual sheep in the care of the Good Shepherd.

It is who the Shepherd is that makes each sheep important.

The Shepherd's Role

Before he was known as Israel's most famous king, David served in obscurity as a shepherd. He saw God's nature in many aspects of shepherding. The most important relationship a sheep has is with its shepherd. The shepherd's job is to gather all the sheep and build a dwelling place for them that keeps death outside the gate. The shepherd prepares the pasture. He pours oil on the ground to keep snakes away, and over the sheeps' heads to keep the bugs away. The shepherd prepares the fields so the sheep can rest.

The shepherd is loyal. The shepherd keeps watch at night. The shepherd keeps watch in the day. The sheep are never left unattended. The shepherd guards the gate so the sheep stay safe from predators. The shepherd rescues his sheep when they head toward a cliff. The shepherd risks his life to protect his sheep. The shepherd is a refuge for the sheep.

The shepherd alone opens the gate and lets the sheep in and out. The sheep hear his voice, and he calls his own sheep by name and leads them out.

If a sheep hears a stranger's voice, it will not follow. Harold Senkbeil, a pastor who grew up as a farmer, shares in his book *The Care of Souls* that the cows on his farm also wouldn't respond to the verbal commands of a stranger, even when they were the exact same commands given with the same intonation as the owner.[7] Isn't that remarkable? We too were made to listen for one voice and respond to that one voice.

After the shepherd leads his sheep out, he walks in front of them, and the sheep follow (John 10:2–4). He paves the way. He sees the valleys and crags ahead before the sheep walk the path. What sweet safety.

> Jesus again said to them, "Truly, truly, I say to you, I am the door of the sheep. All who came before me are thieves and robbers, but the sheep did not listen to them. I am the door. If anyone enters by me, he will be saved and will go in and out and find pasture. The thief comes only to steal and kill and destroy. I came that they may have life and have it abundantly. I am the good shepherd. The good shepherd lays down his life for the sheep." (vv. 7–11)

Do you want to experience peace? Do you want true safety? You will not find it through your personality. Your unique traits, values, emotional patterns, interests, and abilities will never have the power to ground you in safety and rest. You will only find it in your Shepherd. You cannot protect yourself by working on your weaknesses or exploiting your strengths.

The Lord Is My Shepherd

What are your anxieties and fears today? What are the questions that torment you?

Will I ever repair this relationship?

Will I ever be able to crawl out from under the crushing burden of debt?

Where will I go to college?

Will I ever get married?

Will my parents ever love me?

Will I ever break the clutches of postpartum depression?

Why can't I be more desirable?

Will I ever get the respect I deserve at work?

Will I ever be free from my addiction?

Will I ever be able to get through a day without a drink?

How did I get into this unhealthy relationship?

Why can't I be more interesting?

What is it about me that made my spouse cheat on me?

What's wrong with me?

Consider the question of why your spouse would cheat on you, for instance. If we try to wrestle with our spouse's infidelity through the lens of personality, we might uncover reasons why our personalities don't fit, or how his or her personality might have made them prone to infidelity, or how our personality might have made us susceptible to not offer what our spouse felt was needed. These questions might bring some clarity, but they are insufficient to explain another person's sin, and they certainly do not offer rest. They can't make us whole again.

Pause and reflect on whatever question resonates most with you, and consider how to answer that question through the lens of your identity as your personality. The answers are unsatisfying, aren't they? Even if there were enough about yourself you could change to make everything okay, think of the anxiety that effort would induce. Do you see how understanding your identity as your personality cannot offer adequate answers to these questions?

Anxious questions lurk like a whirlpool, threatening to pull us in. When our focus is on these anxious waters, God becomes small. When we focus on ourselves as the answer to these anxious questions, God becomes smaller still. If we trust in a small God, then the waves of these questions will drown us.

Turn your eyes to the only one who can pull you out of the waters of anxiety: the Good Shepherd. Pause and lift up your request to the Lord. Don't filter what you ask or bring only the hard things. Remember, he sees you, hears you, knows you, and delights when you come to him with every request. Psalm 23 reminds us that in the midst of our anxieties, the Lord *is* our Shepherd.

Because the Lord *is*—I can rest. God never sleeps nor slumbers. He always goes before me. He is the only one who can take my whole being—heart, soul, mind, and strength—to the perfectly still waters of true rest.

Because the Lord *is*—I can rest.

Sheep are dependent creatures. They have no claws, no sting in their tail, no sharp teeth to ward off predators. The shepherd is the only one who can provide protection.

Because the Lord *is*—I can trust that he goes before me like a shepherd goes before his sheep to prepare the pasture. Even if I follow him on a path of suffering, I can rest in the confidence that Jesus, my Shepherd, has already walked the path. I don't have to live under the power of my anxieties. He sets my table and protects me, especially when enemies lurk. My true Shepherd protects me from the enemies that seek to kill and destroy me. They don't get the final victory. The Lamb that was slain does. I have permission to walk in the steps that Christ has prepared before me today. The Good Shepherd invites me to follow behind him into today rather than fight to strive through it in my own strength. My Shepherd prepares the land I am called to dwell in and equips me for today's challenges. Striving ceases when we learn to trust and rest in our Shepherd's care for us. I often ask the Lord, "Jesus, what are you inviting me into in this moment?" He bids me to pause and listen.

Because the Lord *is*—I can find peace even when I am in a shadowed valley, because the Lord my Shepherd is *with* me. My Shepherd walked through the blackest night of death and the dominion of evil, straight on, so that we only have to walk through their insubstantial shadow. And he joins us in that shadowed walk. Even death is safe with our Shepherd because it brings us to heaven with him.

Because the Lord *is*—I can rest in the true gift of having God's goodness and mercy follow me all the days of my life. Not only does Jesus lead me forward under his protection as my true Shepherd, but his goodness and steadfast love follow me. Whenever we face trials, we can be assured he will protect us. When our hearts grow weary, we know his compassion toward us does not waver. Even when I walk through trials, his mercy is present. As long as I am his, I am promised he will never leave nor forsake me. When we follow the Good Shepherd, we will find release from the anxiety of our own pressure to change and perform.

The Sheep's Role

Sheep spend a third of their lives grazing. They aren't busy. They are made to graze, not hurry. What about us? We are made to feast at God's table, feast on his Word: "He makes me lie down in green pastures."

My husband admits that he struggles with this. If productivity were a spiritual gift, he would have it in spades. He loves the satisfaction of a fruitful day. And what does he consider fruitful? A day that ends with something to show for his hard work. There is nothing wrong with productivity. In fact, there can be a lot of good in Christ-exalting and gospel-empowered hard work. But what about Christ-exalting and gospel-empowered *rest*? Do we trust there is as much good in a slow-paced day marked by nothing more than good conversations with our family and friends, time in the Word, and time in prayer? According to John's StrengthsFinder results, he's dominated by strategic strengths. Viewed through that lens, a restful day wouldn't be living out his best strengths. But maybe a day of rest is a day when he experiences something even better: his identity as a sheep in the Shepherd's fold.

Can you articulate the whys to all that you do? For example, are you performing to be known? In high school, I was never comfortable resting in the Shepherd's care. I stayed busy. I sought to be known by doing. I made sure I never felt lonely. Blaming my extrovert personality made this easy to get away with. I didn't learn how to rest, let alone to value rest. This poor habit fueled what would later become a heart of discontentment in marriage and in ministry. That discontentment grew into anger and even hatred. When, later in my life, suffering entered my story, my eyes weren't on my Shepherd; my eyes were on myself. I hated God because of what he allowed. My focus was on my pastures, my path, and myself.

Have you ever used your personality as an excuse to stay busy?

"I am an achiever; I'm made to work." "I am a peacemaker; who else is going to fix this conflict?" "I am an investigator; someone has to uncover the truth."[8] Overidentification with personality traits tends to make us take on responsibilities that are not ours. This busyness, in turn, can become a mask for pain.

A blend of busyness and loneliness creates a nasty concoction. Going into full-time ministry after seminary, I became a "yes person." I said yes to most opportunities that were offered to me. I said yes to hosting regular church gatherings, houseguests, and social events in our home; to helping out in our kids' classrooms; to leading the benevolence team and organizing the donut ministry at church. All the while, I lived in a world where I cut myself off from true relationships. I was seen but not known. I served but refused to be served. Busyness that is disconnected from spiritual and emotional health poisons us with frustration, which turns into anger, which turns into hatred. Our souls grow sick. It wasn't until I gave myself permission to admit I was sick that I could place my dependence on my Shepherd and ask him to transform my heart. As a counselor, I've met so many who can't see their disease. They've lived ill so long that sickness feels normal and right.

Busyness can become a mask for pain.

Part of my role as a counselor is to help counselees become mindful of a heart condition they aren't aware of. We spend so much of our energy trying to cure our sickness, but most of us only know the symptoms of that disease, not the underlying cause or proper diagnosis. Our only hope is our Shepherd, who can diagnose the sickness and cure our souls with his intimate care. Counselors, authors, pastors, and godly friends are important guides on this trip, but they are helpers. They shouldn't be confused with the Great Physician of our souls.

Psychological pain is often the result of our lack of wholeness. We experience pain because we don't understand whose we are, and then we mask that pain with activity, trying to make ourselves better in our own eyes. We protect ourselves instead of allowing our Shepherd to be our comfort. It's a vicious cycle. I counsel many who are stuck on this merry-go-round. If hurts are never dealt with, they get buried inside us and rot, only to be unearthed in the future. What is in the dark will always come to light. Why, you might ask? Because there is only room for one person on the throne of our hearts. When we self-protect, we position ourselves on our throne, and Jesus loves us too much to let us stay there.

Have you ever felt a deep sense of loneliness in a roomful of people? Do you notice an internal struggle in this space? Do you crave to be heard, to be known, to be valued? Personality types promise us that we can be known and valued for who we are as defined by our type. But then the yoke of exemplifying and perfecting that personality type is placed on us. And that weight can compound our sense of isolation.

Until we find satisfaction in who Jesus says we are and experience rest in our true identity as sheep, we will constantly battle the need to prove ourselves to others. The pursuit of others' approval often clouds our ability to see how we are already heard, known, and valued by our Shepherd in the most intimate of ways. Seeking the approval of the world is too heavy a burden to bear.

Sheep Know How to Rest

There is a reason sheep aren't beasts of burden. Can you imagine a sheep under the care of a good shepherd pressing past the point of exhaustion, its tiny legs bowed under an enormous burden? Certainly not. There is a reason in Psalm 23 that God tells us we are sheep, not horses or camels. Jesus even tells us to take *his* yoke upon us, a yoke of kindness in exchange for the wearisome yoke we wear.

He promises that in so doing, "you will find rest for your souls. For my yoke is easy, and my burden is light" (Matt. 11:29–30).

God makes us, as his sheep, lie down in green pastures. He leads us beside still waters. He restores our souls. He neither lets us wander aimlessly nor presses us into constant, debilitating work. We find rest in his presence, and only in his presence. Rest is the antidote to the nasty concoction of busyness and loneliness that many of us are gulping down. Rest is the opposite of a wasted life.

Pause. Reflect. Listen.

You are loved and known. Your value comes from him. You don't have to get caught up in the endless cycle of wanting, because Jesus knows your needs and promises to provide for them. You don't need to worry about creating your own path, because your Shepherd is leading you. He prepares the land for you before you enter it (Prov. 16:9). You don't need to be anxious about tomorrow because he knows what tomorrow holds. You don't have to fight through weariness; you can trust him and lie down. You don't have to be afraid, because your Shepherd is with you and will comfort you. You can cast off shame because only your Shepherd has the power to define you, and he has prepared a place for you in the presence of your enemies.[9]

Being his sheep is a gift.

Is your god small? Or is he the Lord, the Good Shepherd? Is he enough for you? If he is and you believe who he says he is, then you must believe who he says you are—a sheep in need of guidance, willing to follow. You can't have one without the other.

Sheep Take the Shepherd's Path

We are the Lord's sheep not just in rest but also in activity. "He *leads* me beside still waters. . . . He *leads* me in paths of righteousness for his name's sake. . . . Even though I walk through the valley of the shadow of death" (emphasis mine). God leads us and calls us to follow. No sheep is self-made. No sheep is self-directed. The activity of sheep is not determined by the sheep's preferences or personality but by what the shepherd thinks is best for the sheep.

Identifying our personality type as our core identity misdirects us not just because it calls us to doing over being, and action over rest, but also because it causes us to misunderstand what God calls us to. My deepest fulfillment comes not from being true to myself but from being obedient to my Shepherd. The Shepherd may even call us to do something that is an apparent mismatch with our personality type. His goal is not our comfort; his goal is our sanctification under his perfect care. His goal is to have us look more and more like him—more loving, more patient, kinder, gentler, and less anxious.

My deepest fulfillment comes not from being true to myself but from being obedient to my Shepherd.

Consider Moses, who tried to weasel himself out of God's call for him because of his introversion. If we were to optimize our lives based on our personality types, our introversion might have us stop evangelizing and hosting dinner parties. Or our extroversion might have us skip quiet times of reflection. But Scripture clearly mandates both. If our Shepherd leads us in those paths of righteousness, we should follow.

John would say he is not naturally gifted as a counselor or caregiver. Yet he finds that his Shepherd regularly leads him into the valley of the shadow of death alongside those in hospice care. He bids John to follow not because of his natural proclivities or giftings but because that is God's calling on John's life. I am not naturally gifted as a writer, yet here I am, writing a book with John, not because of my gifting but because Christ intended me to be faithful to steward the good he has for me.

Paul knew what it was to have God press him outside his natural giftings. He spent much of his ministry obediently speaking, even though that was not a strength of his (1 Cor. 2:3–5; 2 Cor. 10:10). Later, Paul confessed that God seemed particularly delighted to invite him to obedience in his weakness. When God told him, "My grace is sufficient for you, for my power is made perfect in weakness," Paul responded, "Therefore I will boast all the more gladly of my weaknesses, so that the power of Christ may rest upon me. For the sake of Christ, then, I am content with weaknesses, insults, hardships, persecutions, and calamities. For when I am weak, then I am strong" (2 Cor. 12:9–10). Your Shepherd may call you to obedience in areas outside your strengths for his good purposes, for your sake, and to bring glory to himself.

Sheep Know Their Shepherd

Our Shepherd provides protection, safety, and direction: "I am the good shepherd. I know my own and my own know me, just as the Father knows me and I know the Father; and I lay down my life for the sheep" (John 10:14–15). Our Shepherd withholds nothing from us, not even his own life. We can trust him because he knows us, he has walked our path, and he has given himself for us. Every step you take today is one ordained by your perfect Shepherd. That means he has an invitation for you in every encounter, every conversation, and every battle. Find rest in knowing that nothing is a surprise to God, and wherever you are today, he has anointed, appointed, and equipped you to step into his righteousness.

Maybe you find yourself needing to say yes to someone or something. Or perhaps you need to say no. Whatever your circumstance, he delights in giving every ounce of the courage, trust, faith, conviction, and peace you need on this particular day. Lean in. Know the One who provides it all. Rest, little sheep. All you have is today. Your Shepherd knows your tomorrow. Just be faithful today.

To know ourselves, then, we must first know our Shepherd. And when we know our Shepherd, we will begin to know ourselves. Our personalities become unique secondary attributes given to us by our Shepherd, to be used for his glory. Rest and be with your Shepherd, fellow sheep.

PRAYER

My Great Shepherd, thank you for calling me your own. Though I feel overwhelmed, give me wisdom with my next steps. Lead me in your mercy and grace. Quiet my soul to trust in your sovereignty and goodness.

Even in the madness I find myself in, you have purpose for me. Forgive my self-focus. Forgive my efforts to define myself primarily through my personality traits. I trust that you are for me, that you are with me, and that I will not walk this journey alone. Speak to me, Lord. Let my heart be awakened by the mystery of your love. Fill the silence with your voice. Teach me how to be your sheep. Teach me to listen. Break me of whatever gets in the way. I need you, my Good Shepherd. Amen.

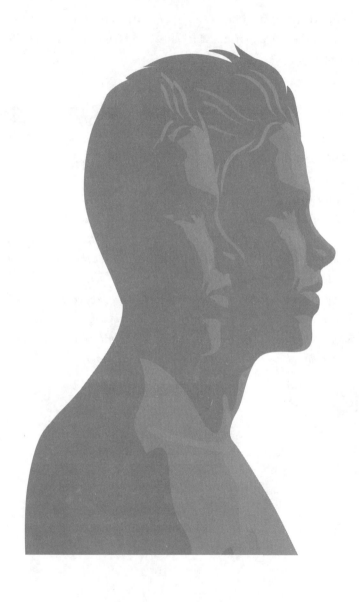

Desires
Finding Satisfaction as a Saint

⁓

You have no rights in our lovemaking.
—Derek Jarman

I think choosing between men and women is like choosing between cake and ice cream. You'd be daft not to try both when there are so many different flavors.
—Björk

You are the light of the world.
—Jesus

JOHN

"GOD MADE ME LIKE THIS. He wouldn't want me to be unhappy." The woman across from Angel crossed her arms, holding in her assertion. Angel leaned forward and asked, "What did he make you for?" She responded, growing in despair, "How can a good God make me a sexual being, tell me that he is good and that my sexuality is good, and then tell me I can't pursue my desires for sex?"

☞

Angel sat across from another woman who had finally acknowledged her addiction to sugar. It had led to diabetes. She longs for freedom from her desire for sugar but fears losing the comfort it brings. She can't imagine a day without a Twix.

☞

"What did you want to share with me?" I asked the young man facing me in his chair. Brandon exhaled and launched in: "I still remember that sleepover at my friend's house. I was in eighth grade and, over pizza and Cokes by the pool, my friends started talking about girls they had crushes on. As I listened to them share about the girls they thought were cute, I felt a sense of dread creep over me as I knew they would eventually ask me who I had a crush on. The truth was that I had feelings for a friend of mine who was sitting right next to me. When they pressed me about who I thought was cute, I mentioned a girl at school and was relieved when they didn't press too hard for more details. I've never had those kinds of feelings for girls."

☞

Desires drive us. We wake up craving a cup of coffee. We feel compelled to scroll through social media. We long to go on that Caribbean cruise our friends went on last year. We hate our kitchen and want a Chip and Joanna Gaines–inspired remodel. We yearn to be loved.

We feel. We long. We crave.

What could possibly be wrong with someone pursuing their desires?

Our culture fans the flame of our desires. We are surrounded by messages that we will be satisfied if we just eat this food, drive that vehicle, go on that vacation, win this bet, drink that beverage, or feel this person's touch. It is not surprising that cultural norms regarding sexuality have dramatically shifted. We are invited to explore any desire we have.

The world says: What you desire defines who you are. But does that definition really bring us the freedom we long for?

Love Is Love?

Do you remember your first crush? Who can forget the first romantic feelings that stirred inside us? It is intoxicating to want to be with someone, and more intoxicating still to have them want to be with us.

"Love is love." What does that mean? Much of the cultural shift pivots on that truism. The "love is love" slogan holds incredible power. How can we deny it? On the one hand, we cannot. After all, "love is love" is a tautology—that is, a statement that is true and yet does not give the hearer any additional information; for instance, "The ice is frozen" or "She was a dark-brown-haired brunette." The redundancy in these statements makes them devoid of persuasive power. Other than the self-evident, we have no information when you tell us you saw the sunrise in the morning.

Yet the tautology "love is love" holds incredible sway in the West. This is because at the heart of this statement lies the belief that our desires are essential to our identity. What is being smuggled into the supposed truism is that any type of sexual attraction is love. The first "love" in "love is love" references sexual desire; the second love references the universal emotion of affectionate commitment to another.

It is understandable that we want to equate something as powerful as love to our identity. What could be more essential to our humanity than love?

We recently saw a social media post by someone celebrating thirty-eight years of marriage. The wife shared that when she was fifteen, she and her twenty-year-old boyfriend eloped to a state where it was legal for them to marry despite her parents' objections. How do you feel about that story? Should we unabashedly celebrate along with this couple? If you have a teenage daughter like us, you might feel more than a little conflicted. We want to cheer on the abiding love this couple has for one another. We honor their commitment. We want to celebrate the fact that they defied the odds. And yet, isn't there a part of you that wonders how pure her husband's intentions were at the time? How many fifteen-year-old girls are able to make a lifelong commitment? If laws allowed for fifteen-year-old girls to marry men of any age, wouldn't you get a little concerned about male predators who might take advantage of adolescent girls?

Inside most of us there is some degree of check to any person's living out what they might call love in every circumstance.

Most of us acknowledge that not all desires are necessarily good. Not all desires for food are good, whether in type or quantity. Not all desires for power are good. Our desire for comfort can be problematic if it leads us to become a couch potato. And sexual desires aren't intrinsically good. We all have lines we believe should not be crossed: sexual desire for animals, for children, for violence, for non-consensual intercourse. The question is, how do we redraw these lines when we act on desires that are problematic or even perverse?

The fact that a line exists between good and malformed desires ought to tip us off that it is unwise to root our identity in our desires.

In my experience as a pastor and Angel's as a counselor, we have met with many who have conflated their identity with their desires: "I am gay." "I am a gamer." "I am an alcoholic." "I am an addict." Even the statement "I am fat" or "I am beautiful no matter my size" can refer to a mindset regarding desires more than one's physiology. When we identify with our desires, we've allowed them to define us and acquiesced to their power over us. And let's be clear: desire is never fulfilled. It always wants more, leaving our core identities void of the solid ground of being enough.

What if we are not defined by our desires but are designed to have our desires transformed by our Creator? What if they are to emerge from our identity in love himself: God? First John 4:8 asserts that "God is love." So is love the same thing as my desire—or is love defined by God?

Love Might *Not* Be Love

What then is love?

Our culture believes love is defined by what we desire. But the epistle of James warns us to handle desire more cautiously: "Each person is tempted when he is lured and enticed by his own desire" (1:14). James continues, explaining the consequences of capitulating: "Desire when it has conceived gives birth to sin, and sin when it is fully grown brings forth death" (v. 15).

If "God is love," as John says, then the Author of life, not our desires, defines what true love is. That being the case, what we call love might not be love at all. And the reputation of God is at stake when we label "love" what isn't love.

Angel is known for her commitment to healthy eating. She believes healthy food is important because it impacts our health and how we feel. If our son, Soren, grabbed Twinkies and a Coke from the vending machine at school at lunch every day, that would break Angel's heart, because she cares for him. But it would be worse still if Soren stuck a couple of dollars into the machine for a Twinkie and Coke every day, then told his friends, "This is exactly how my mom wants me to spend my money. She says Twinkies and Coke will make me healthy and strong." Soren's behavior now would not only harm him, but it would also negatively impact Angel's reputation. Even worse, because Soren used her credibility to justify his actions, he might potentially harm his friends as well.

So please enjoy and celebrate God's good gifts, such as love and laughter and lava cake. But we are never justified in allowing the gift to be our preeminent focus. In fact, Scripture never uses the terminology of love for things.

> **Enjoy and celebrate God's good gifts. But we are never justified in allowing the gift to be our preeminent focus.**

Still, the Bible has a very broad net for love: a parent's love for a child, siblings' love for each other, friends' love for one another, the love of those in the church for one another. The Gospels clearly portray Jesus's brotherly love for John, Peter, and Lazarus, among others.

God wants us to experience love in all forms, but our culture tends to flatten the expressions of love to just one: romantic love.

So let's pause here and examine this particularly sticky desire. The Bible tells us that God has given boundaries to the expression of sexual love. Let's confine our argument to just what Jesus and Paul say.[1] When addressing the issue of marriage and divorce, Jesus appeals to Genesis 2:

> Have you not read that he who created them from the beginning made them male and female, and said, "Therefore a man shall leave his father and his mother and hold fast to his wife, and the two shall become one flesh"? So they are

no longer two but one flesh. What therefore God has joined together, let not man separate." (Matt. 19:4–6)

Jesus points back to the created order and God's purpose in creating Adam and Eve for one another. Their marriage was not just an accident but a demonstration of what God intended sexual love to be: one man and one woman made one flesh by God until death. God has purposed our sexuality for the marital bed, Jesus asserts.

Paul emphasizes Jesus's interpretation of Genesis 2 in Ephesians 5:22–32, where he explains that God purposes the one man-one woman union to be a picture of Jesus's relationship with the church. The reason for the guardrails God has given us not only relate to what is best for us but also to what God has intended from all eternity: for the marriage of a man and a woman to reflect the love Jesus has for his people.

Because our sexuality is intended to point to Christ's love for the church in the context of marriage (see chapter 6 for a fuller explanation of why this is), Paul includes both homosexual practice and sex outside of marriage as sins in his lists of what displeases God (Rom. 1:18–31; 1 Cor. 10:6–14; Gal. 5:19–21; 1 Tim. 1:8–11). Note that in his lists Paul includes a host of sins that we tend to diminish: covetousness, envy, strife, deceit, maliciousness, gossiping, foolishness, faithlessness, lying, grumbling, idolatry, fits of anger, divisiveness, and drunkenness. All these sins are misdirected desires taking reign in our lives. They displease God and do not reflect his character. Paul's statement in Galatians 5:21 sums up the fate of those who live lives characterized by gratifying the desires of the flesh: they "will not inherit the kingdom of God."

As Westerners, we have an aversion to this strong language. It doesn't fit with how we expect a loving God to act. How could God not allow us to do what we want to do? Perhaps our definition of love needs to be examined.

God Is Love

If God is love, doesn't he want us to experience love? Certainly. Since God is love, and God wants us to experience him, it is logical that God wants us to experience love. And his love is far better and deeper and truer than any love we can experience in this world. In Jesus's final words to his apostles, he says, "As the Father has loved me, so have I loved you. Abide in my love" (John 15:9). He invites all of us into the perfect love Jesus experiences with the Father. Stop and think about that for a minute. Jesus loves all of us like he loves God the Father. How crazy big is that love? There's nothing that can make him stop loving us.

God's love is unconditional, but at the same time it also directs us toward our sanctification and obedience. God didn't love Angel less in her season of adultery. Even when she refused to repent, she still felt convicted in her sin. In his relentless love for her, he never stopped pursuing her heart. The twinge in Angel's heart that told her she was abusing grace brought deeper conviction that she ought not take advantage of his long-suffering patience toward her. In the mire, she prayed over and over again, "God convict me, no matter the cost." In his mercy, God eventually brought a spirit of brokenness that led to her repentance. She was moved to want to love and obey him in return. Angel shares that his love for her now moves her to call others to repentance in truth and in love. It is a significant part of her counseling practice. Sobriety of heart, soul, mind, and strength is found through the path of repentance.

God's love is unconditional, but it also directs us toward our sanctification and obedience.

Angel's experience mirrors Jesus's promise to us. "If you keep my commandments, you will abide in my love, just as I have kept my Father's commandments and abide in his love" (John 15:10). We abide as we obey. We plunge ourselves deeper into the heart of God as we entrust ourselves to his will and not our own and submit our desires to his desires. The lie the world sells is that if we achieve our desires, we'll be happy. But our yearning hearts only want more and more, dragging us into a dark well of scarcity.

While there is legitimacy to most of our desires (for instance, to experience intimacy, comfort, or respect or to make an impact), nevertheless, when we make these desires ultimate, they twist our hearts to the Enemy's dark purposes. Before we know what's happening, we're trapped in dank underground catacombs, chasing our desires around the next corner and the next until we're hopelessly lost. Consider the pursuit of respect. The desire to be esteemed can lead to cutting corners, lying, power grabs, and workaholism. Every person deserves to be respected, but when we make that appropriate longing a controlling desire in our life, it leads our hearts along shadowy paths.

When Angel felt like she lost control is most areas of her life, she sought to gain control of her health. She was at the gym every morning when it opened. There were some good things about this pursuit—a healthier body, for one—but her desire for control, health, and intimacy opened the door to inappropriate and unhealthy attachments. "I can handle it" was a regular response in her inner monologue:

Can we afford a membership at the expensive gym? "I can handle it."
Can we afford a personal trainer? "I can handle it."
Can I respect the boundaries of a relationship with a male personal trainer? "I can handle it."
Can I stop this trainer's romantic pursuit of me? "I can handle it."

Angel shares today, "I couldn't handle it."

"I can handle it" is a lie that grants our desires power, and when we give our desires power over us, they lead us toward self-destruction.

How can we be freed from the siren call of our desires? It's clear, even outside of Scripture, that contentment is the key to freedom. And contentment is found in trust.

When we give our desires power over us, they lead us toward self-destruction.

Trusting in God's love is trusting that he will meet you in his love —and more. It's also trusting he will give you both the true desires of your heart and truly loving relationships in this world. God delights in having his love for us expressed through relationships: parental, friendship, and romantic. In the scope of the Bible, there are many more examples of God's love through friendship than through romantic love. While the latter is not ignored, the Bible invites us into a fuller vision of friendship than many Westerners have. God has purposed us for deep and meaningful relationships with our families (though, unfortunately, some don't experience this love). God gives us the gift of committed love between friends. And God gives some of us the opportunity to experience his love through romantic love.

But there are parameters.

If God is love, why doesn't God allow us to do anything we want? Wouldn't that be loving? Any parent knows that isn't the case. A loving mom doesn't allow her strong-willed three-year-old to tear off across the street just because he wants to. A caring dad doesn't cave to his third grader's declaration, "I don't like homework, so I'm not doing it anymore." God's ultimate love is demonstrated in this: that he gave his Son for us so we might be like him. God's love doesn't permit; it transforms.

What does transformative love change our desirous hearts into? Saints.

What Is a Saint?

"I'm no saint." The statement betrays our culture's perception of what a saint is.

What do you think of when you think of a saint? We're guessing it involves a halo, head bowed, and palms lightly pressed together in prayer or outward in supplication. We're guessing Saint Teresa of Calcutta or Saint Mary or Saint Francis come to mind.

Our culture thinks only the most elite Christians make it to sainthood. Saints are the Navy SEAL Team Six; saints are the Delta Force of Christians. To be a saint requires not just being virtuous but being heroic. In fact, some branches of Christianity even require you to have independently verified miracles (plural!) on your resume.

If that's what a saint is, then Angel and I will add our voices to the crowd: we're no saints.

But is that what a saint is? The New Testament paints a very different picture of sainthood.

The term *saint* appears eighty-two times in the New Testament, but not a single time does its usage denote someone who is set apart from other Christians as sort of a Christian-plus or a summa-cum-laude Christian.

Paul uses the term eight times just in his letter to the church at Rome. He begins it, "To all those in Rome who are loved by God and called to be *saints*: Grace to you and peace from God our Father and the Lord Jesus Christ" (Rom. 1:7, my emphasis).

Later, Paul talks about the call of the church to care for Christians in need both within their church (12:13) and in the church at Jerusalem (15:25–26). He refers to both groups of Christians as saints.

Paul begins both of his letters to the church at Corinth (which, parenthetically, was a group of Christians who had profound struggles in their faithfulness) in much the same way: "To the church of God that is in Corinth, to those sanctified in Christ Jesus, called to be saints together with all those who in every place call upon the name of our Lord Jesus Christ" (1 Cor. 1:2). And again, "Paul, an apostle of Christ Jesus by the will of God, and Timothy our brother, To the church of God that is at Corinth, with all the saints who are in the whole of Achaia" (2 Cor. 1:1).

Paul's letter to the church at Ephesus begins with the same language: "Paul, an apostle of Christ Jesus by the will of God, To the saints who are in Ephesus, and are faithful in Christ Jesus" (Eph. 1:1).

And to the church at Philippi: "To all the saints in Christ Jesus who are at Philippi, with the overseers and deacons" (Phil. 1:1).

And to the church at Colossae: "To the saints and faithful brothers in Christ at Colossae: Grace to you and peace from God our Father" (Col. 1:2).

Paul refers to Christians as saints also in Thessalonians, Timothy, and Philemon. And just so it's clear that this is not just a quirk of Paul's, we also find the author of Hebrews closes with a greeting to the saints: "Greet all your leaders and all the saints" (Heb. 13:24). And we find Jude begins his letter refering to all Christians: "I found it necessary to write appealing to you to contend for the faith that was once for all delivered to the saints" (Jude v. 3). In the book of Acts, Luke refers to ordinary Christians as saints (9:13, 32, 41; 26:10). And in the book of Revelation, John refers to Christians as saints as well (Rev. 5:8).

A saint, quite simply, is a Christian.[2] A saint is someone who has been transformed from unholy to holy, from unrighteous to righteous. If you have trusted Christ, you are a saint. Christ has taken your sins on himself on the cross and imputed his righteousness to you (planting it in your heart), and in the power of the Spirit your desires are conformed to his pure desires.

> **A saint, quite simply, is a Christian—someone who has been transformed from unholy to holy, from unrighteous to righteous.**

As saints we receive our new status as transformed and reborn followers of God. We are those who have been made into the likeness of God's love. Our identity, then, isn't rooted in our conception of love but in God's. Our identity isn't found in our sexuality but in the Author of love.

Know Your Sainthood

In middle school Angel was teased for being good. Her name made her an easy target. A classmate used to mock her with a song to the tune of "Nanny Nanny Boo Boo." He would greet any misstep of hers with, "Angel got her wings cut off." But she wasn't the only one. The kids at my middle school dubbed me "Saint John."

This mocking was intended to make us feel embarrassed for being serious about our faith. And to some extent, the teasing worked. We both felt a measure of shame and embarrassment that we wouldn't do what the cool kids did.

Today, as our teenagers have experienced some of the same pressure and teasing from their friends, we have tried to emphasize to them the joy of their sainthood. Being a saint is something to celebrate! Saints are those who reflect the purity of God's heart to a world longing for goodness. As saints we have the choice not to run after fading desires. True satisfaction is found in obeying, even if it doesn't feel fun. Jesus warns us, "This is the judgment: the light has come into the world, and people loved the darkness rather than the light because their works were evil" (John 3:19). Because of Christ at work in us, saints run toward the light and flee darkness.

Imagine that you are gifted an Armani suit or a Dolce & Gabbana dress. You put on the suit or the dress, and you look better than you've ever looked. Where do you go? Somewhere special, right? You don't walk downtown, slide a cover off a manhole, and jump down into the sewer!

To follow Jesus is to not jump in the sewer. When we live in the power of our flesh, we cannot help but be drawn to the world. By the power of the Spirit at work within us, we can run toward the light. As saints, we can walk in the manner in which we were called. We can pursue righteousness. We have the ability to run away from sin, live by faith, and pursue good.

And yet, sainthood is so much more about the positive power of the pure than it is the negative power of the dark. Why focus on staying out of the sewer when we can focus on the banquet God has for us?

Throughout Scripture, God's work in our lives is connected with light.

Oftentimes, when preachers talk about light, the analogy is explained this way: We are the moon reflecting the light of the sun. There is powerful truth in this explanation. We are not, of course, the source of light.

But incredibly, that analogy doesn't go far enough. Both Jesus and Paul insist that we *are* light (Matt. 5:14; Phil. 2:15). In the Sermon on the Mount, Jesus tells us we are a light in a dark room (Matt. 5:15–16). In Ephesians, Paul tells us that while we used to be darkness, we are now light. In 1 John, John encourages us that "the darkness is passing away and the true light is already shining" (1 John 2:8). Our natures have been transformed. In Christ, our identity is no longer the identity of darkness; it is the identity of light. We have the Holy Spirit within us, the third person of the one true and living God, who is himself the essence of light.

There is truth in the moon analogy insofar as we understand that we ourselves do not *create* the light within us. But the power of the Spirit within every follower of Jesus is greater than a mere reflective power; we are by our very nature *light*. Every Christian is a saint. God created us to shine in the darkness, to be the light that draws other people from the sewer to the gorgeous banquet he's prepared. It is who we are as children of the "Father of lights" (James 1:17). When we pursue the things of the flesh, we are fighting who God has transformed us to be.

When we pursue the things of the flesh, we are fighting who God has transformed us to be.

So for us to live in a manner worthy of the calling we have received means something better than just mustering up the effort; it means we have to *be who we are*. When our daughter interviewed for scholarships at colleges, we sympathized with her temptation to perform or create an image. But we knew her most impactful interview would come from her being most wholly herself: honest, authentic, transparent, joy filled, passionate, not afraid to express her weaknesses when necessary. So it is with us. We most powerfully demonstrate Christ when we are most truly ourselves.

And we are light! When we become children of God, he indwells us with his very own Spirit. God describes himself as light (John 8:12) and his breath gives us life (Job 33:4). Our true nature is that of light. Thus, wherever we go, we get to show the purity, goodness, and truth of God in our lives as saints, because he is truly alive in us. When Christ calls you to himself, it's like God plugs you into his lampstand. Wherever you go in this dark world, his light over you, in you, and through you never diminishes. You are a saint!

When we receive the Lord's declaration that we are saints, we can then step into understanding the value of sainthood. We must believe our relationship with the Lord is more powerful than our relationship with our flesh. We've all experienced the disappointment of pursuing our desires. We've gorged ourselves only to feel terrible in the morning. We've given in to lust only to be filled with regret. We've bought something we didn't really need and then gotten stuck with the credit card bill that far exceeded our joy of the object. Saints, on the other hand, experience the peace and contentment of God's love.

> **Our relationship with the Lord is more powerful than our relationship with our flesh.**

Saints know the freedom of leaving past sin, shame, guilt, anger, and wrongdoing all at the cross and have permission to grow in a sensitivity to the Spirit of the living God inside themselves.

Saints know their home is in glory. That knowledge is perfect motivation to hate sin a little more.

We invite you to value being a saint, because you are made to shine the pure light: goodness, faith, love, and truth. When you receive that truth for yourself, you look for ways to point others to Christ, and the kingdom grows.

What Sainthood Does

Equating our identity with our desires has repercussions. We allow our appetites to define us. We become our own lord.

We aren't intended to be our own master. We can't control much of anything, and the weight of that responsibility is too much for us mere creatures to bear. For instance, while we might set some boundaries in our relationships—monogamy, as an example—we cannot pick and choose the guardrails God has given us for our desires. A monogamous homosexual relationship might more closely reflect God's purpose for romantic love than a casual heterosexual hookup, but we shouldn't delude ourselves that it expresses God's holy design. On a different tack, we might insist we're only concerned about our social media ratings because they're part of our job, but is that really true? How does it express God's heart when our drive for recognition leads us to ignore those around us and neglect making disciples of our neighbors?

In Colossians 1:10–14, Paul prays that we would be enabled to

walk in a manner worthy of the Lord, fully pleasing to him: bearing fruit in every good work and increasing in the knowledge of God; being strengthened with all power, according to his glorious might, for all endurance and patience with joy; giving thanks to the Father, who has qualified you to share in the inheritance of the saints in light. He has delivered us from the domain of darkness and transferred us to the kingdom of his beloved Son, in whom we have redemption, the forgiveness of sins.

In Christ, we have already been delivered. Already!

The degree to which we understand our sainthood is the degree to which we resist living under the power of shame and guilt. There is a lot of weight to that truth. It gives us personal permission not to spend a lifetime fighting to escape pain of the past, or present desires, or false identities that have no lasting peace or bring no eternal assurance. If you are already set free from the bondage of desires turned into sin, then you have the freedom to know your worth as a saint.

If, as the Westminster Shorter Catechism puts it, our purpose for being is to "glorify God and enjoy him forever," then knowing our sainthood gives us the freedom to delight God in living lives worthy of him, fully pleasing to him. The work of the Spirit of God produces fruit that reflects the person of Christ in our lives.

Know Where You Stand

As a saint you have already been given the strength you need today, wherever you are (Isa. 41:10).

As a saint you have the power to live a life that is pleasing, pure, and purposeful. This righteous life is one that flees from sin, pursues good, and lives by faith (1 Cor. 6:18–20).

As a saint you can find joy and gratitude in a life that denies the flesh and welcomes the Spirit (Luke 9:23).

As a saint you stand with all the other saints! You stand next to Paul, Matthew, and Mark. You stand next to Timothy and Mary, Martha and Ruth. And one day you will get to enjoy a meal next to them and hear about how God showed his faithfulness in their lives. You are set apart in an eternal, life-giving holiness that leads us into worship. You already have a place in heaven. Can you anticipate the goodness that awaits? Straighten your crown and live into your royal purity.

As a saint you are set free from darkness and the weight of desires that dragged you into the sewer of scarcity. Those things don't have the final say over you. You have already been delivered into the kingdom where Jesus reigns. God has transferred his light into you; you are light. As a saint you no longer live for yourself.

Perhaps your desire for food controls your thought life. You spend your time between meals snacking and imagining the meal to come. You hate your body, but you feel like you need the chips in the pantry after you've eaten a full meal.

Perhaps your desire to be in control means you are drawn to codependent relationships. Or your desire to be free from anxiety has led to a dependence on marijuana. You can't remember the last day you didn't smoke a joint.

Maybe you want to watch porn, or have sex with your significant other, or enter a same-sex relationship, or cohabitate with your fiancé. But what would Jesus invite you to do? Jesus looks at us in love and asks us to trust him and submit our desires to his desires. He invites us to release control of our lives and hand over the title of Master to him. One of the most powerful ways we have seen trust in Jesus proclaimed through the lives of our friends who experience same-sex attraction is through their choice to walk the path of celibacy and purity.

Jesus looks at us in love and asks us to trust him and submit our desires to his desires.

For those of you who struggle with desires outside of God's purposes, hear the gracious invitation from your Creator. Look to heaven, fellow saints. Pray that God would grant you a soul-rattling desire for "a better country" (Heb. 11:16). Pray that your desires would not be satisfied by this world. Ask that God would give you a thirst that only he can satiate (John 4:13–14). There awaits us a life for all eternity with no sin, no shame, no guilt, and no suffering. Our hearts will be perfectly aligned with God's desires.

As saints we are satisfied as we hunger and thirst for righteousness. This isn't to say that we will never struggle with sin and the desires of our flesh, but we have power over the flesh through God's love. Theologian Kelly Kapic says, "A pious and holy person is not one who is free from the struggle with sin but one who freely soaks in the love of the Father and the grace of the Son and finds renewal in the strong fellowship of the Spirit."[3] The struggle reveals our saintliness. The struggle calls us to trust in God's grace.

Our desires were given to us to call us to the only One who can fulfill those desires: God himself. Augustine, a fourth-century bishop well acquainted with his own desires, once said, "You have made us for yourself, and our heart is restless until it rests in you."[4] Our desires do not define us. Our desire for food reminds us that Jesus is the only bread that can satisfy (John 6:32–35). Our desire for status reminds us that Jesus calls us his child. Our desire for security reminds us that God is our refuge and strength. Our desire for relationships points us to the truth that Jesus is the only water that can quench our thirst.

Jesus invites us to meet with him in prayer and fully give him our hearts—our emotions, will, and dependency—in order to know him and be known by him. He is enough to satisfy us. Make a choice to open your Bible, sit at his feet, and listen to his voice; reading Scripture out loud can help. Jesus invites us to share our deepest guilt and shame with him and to experience his healing forgiveness. This relationship is the only one that can truly satisfy. Our desires are gifts to be stewarded for our good and to bring God glory. Receiving our desires in this context, as a gift, and knowing they are for our good transforms how we step into loving God, loving others, and appreciating our world. We see others no longer as tools to satisfy our desires but as fellow image bearers. We see creation not as the goal but as signposts that point us to God. We have our understanding of love expanded from the satisfaction of lust to self-giving and others-serving.

God has made us with desires. The author of Ecclesiastes reminds us that our yearning comes from God: "He has put eternity into man's heart" (Eccl. 3:11). But our desires are not our identity. Our longings remind us of our desperate need for God. God meets us in our desires and shapes our desires toward him.

Embrace God's eternal purposes for you today. If you are in Christ, you are a saint. Repent, surrender your desires to him, and make a choice to step into his new mercies for you.

PRAYER

Heavenly Father, forgive me for pursuing my own desires. Forgive me for defending my lusts and making them right in my own eyes. *God, I long to have my heart transformed and to desire only what you desire. Thank you for making me pure, a saint. Thank you for giving me the power to overcome my flesh. Thank you that your love is the only love that satisfies and that you want my best. Make me more like you every day. May my heart's purity reflect your righteousness to this muddied and marred world. I echo Augustine's prayer: "Come, O Lord, and stir our hearts. Call us back to yourself. Kindle your fire in us and carry us away. Let us scent your fragrance and taste your sweetness. Let us love you and hasten to your side."[5] Amen.*

Marriage
Finding Wholeness as the Bride of Christ

⤳

When I design a wedding dress with a bustle, it has to be
one the bride can dance in.
—Vera Wang

Let no man deceive himself. Outside this house, that is,
outside the church, no one is saved.
—Origen of Alexandria

ANGEL

JACK'S ACHING WAS PALPABLE. "I don't know who I am now that she's gone. I'm lost." He had aged a decade in the year and a half his wife had cancer. He lovingly poured everything he had into trying to heal her: his time, his prayers, his finances, his heart. And now she was gone.

Avery looked so put together on the outside—a fresh manicure, perfectly done makeup and hair. But you could hear her voice catch and her eyes moisten when she began to share with me. "My life is wasting away. Why won't God send me a husband? I feel like everything is on pause until I become a wife."

⟋

The wedding reception room was inviting. Candles flickered, swelling piano chords filled the room, faces stretched wide with grins. As I sat at the reception table, my ten-year-old eyes never left the bride. She was beautiful—the embodiment of everything I hoped for. She was marrying a young pastor at our church. I prayed, "Jesus, please let me be a pastor's wife one day."

That night, as our young pastor wed his beautiful bride, my identity was wed with the idea of one day being a bride. The wedding ushered in my obsession with the newly released *Father of the Bride* movie—and any other rom-com that culminated in a wedding. I hammered out every detail of my future wedding, including the bejeweled sneakers worn by Annie (the bride in *Father of the Bride*). My heart, my mind, and my soul were shaped by that day to come. In fact, in sixth grade I made a list of every characteristic I wanted in my future husband and started praying fervently for him.

Who wouldn't want to be in a healthy marriage? We all dream of being in a relationship with someone who knows us, values us, and speaks hope into us. In Hebrew, the first word that refers to sex in the Bible (Gen. 4:1) is *yada*, which also means "to know intimately." We all want to be intimately known.

In one of the most memorable romantic scenes in the history of cinema, sports agent Jerry Maguire (played by Tom Cruise) confesses to his wife (played by Renée Zellweger) that while he was celebrating one of his greatest nights professionally, it felt empty without her. "I love you," Maguire declares. "You complete me."[1]

The flaw in my praying so fervently for all the characteristics I wanted in my future husband was that I was shaping my heart to rely on him to complete me, not the Lord. I was waiting for the day when my knight in shining armor would sweep me off my feet and bring me safety, security, value, worth, and happiness.

We've all been raised with a "you complete me" view of love. We're told, "Your other half is out there waiting for you: the yin to your yang, the peanut butter to your jelly, the wine to your cheese, the bacon to your eggs." Even those who would balk at predestination rely heavily on its language when talking about love. "I found the one!" "We were destined to be together."

We've all been raised with a "you complete me" view of love.

I remember the first time I laid eyes on John. I had just entered high school, and he was the president of the school's Fellowship of Christian Athletes. I went to the lunch meeting on that sunny day in a classroom at Canyon Del Oro High School, and I thought to myself, "*That* is the man I've been praying for!" I prayed for a friendship, and from that friendship, I prayed for a relationship. At that young age, I began making my relationship with John the source of my identity.

This is dangerous territory in a relationship. When we allow our spouse or ideas of a future spouse to be the anchor to which we stake our happiness, value, worth, safety, and security, we set ourselves up for failure in marriage. Our identity is tied to expectations of our other half, which that person was never designed to fulfill.

While the value of matrimony has been chiseled down in our culture, in Christian circles we still hold fast to its importance. And rightly so. Marriage was created to be the most intimate relationship on this earth. In no other relationship do two become one. Christ calls us to love our neighbor as ourselves, and the closest neighbor we ought to have, if we are married, is our spouse.

And yet marriage wasn't meant to be our identity. Rather, it was intended to point to our identity as Christ's bride.

Unfulfilled Expectations

Psychologist Eli Finkel researched changing expectations in marriage and discovered that, compared with previous generations, we Westerners expect our spouses to provide a disproportionate amount of emotional and psychological fulfillment.[2] Just a few generations ago, our expectations for a spouse were modest. Women typically hoped for financial provision and men hoped for a social match, but few expected a close friendship with their spouse. Today we expect our spouse to be our best friend, fulfilling sexual lover, and coparent in raising our children.

Such a match is a beautiful gift, but it places a tremendous burden on our spouse to provide for our happiness. What if God intended us to gain our identity through our marriage to Christ, not through our marriage on earth? What if a core identity we as Christians share is that we are the bride of Christ, not the bride or groom of our spouse? What if trusting Christ to fill that role freed those in marriage to not bear the weight of their spouse's happiness and also ennobled those who were single?

As a young girl I believed the lie that my identity would be fulfilled in my future husband. I longed for the safety and security my future groom would bring. After I married John and he didn't provide everything I needed, that dream shattered, and I went looking for satisfaction elsewhere.

It is a dangerous road when we reject who we are as the bride of Christ and choose to find our identity in a spouse, for they were never designed to fill that role. Your spouse will let you down. No individual human should have the responsibility of completing your identity.

Furthermore, it is dangerous to reject who we are as part of the bride of Christ, because Christ's redemptive work is not merely for the individual; it is collective. The letters in the New Testament are written to instruct followers of Jesus how to live together as part of a collective whole. We will stand together as God's people at the end of history, not only rescued individually but also redeemed together.

Jesus's ministry is communal in nature, and his commandments for the Christian life are weaved into the cloth of the church. To reject his community is to reject Jesus.

To understand this, we must go to the end of the story.

Correcting the End

The end of any book or story is critical to understanding the whole. If you remove the end of The Lord of the Rings where Frodo destroys the ring in Mount Doom; if you closed *The Lion, the Witch and the Wardrobe* right after Aslan is killed by the White Witch; if you stopped watching *The Sixth Sense* before it is revealed that the child's psychologist, Malcolm Crowe, is dead . . . then you would not appreciate the whole story. In fact, master authors make you see every page of the book differently once you have read to the end.

In his book *The King Jesus Gospel*, Scot McKnight argues that evangelicals have minimized Jesus's invitation to join his kingdom to a formula that secures heaven after death. Whether it's fair to paint all of evangelicalism with this critique or not, surveys show this is how many in the United States perceive Christianity. Many believe that mere assent to Jesus's death and resurrection provides the gate code to heaven. But Scripture says that even demons acknowledge that Jesus is Lord (Matt. 8:29; James 2:19). Acknowledging Jesus is the Son of God obviously doesn't guarantee entrance into the kingdom of God.

The traditional idea is that we arrive at the pearly gates and Peter thumbs through our file, finds we have accepted Jesus as our Savior, then nods and lets us in so we can sit on a cloud and strum a harp. In this fraudulent picture, we enter heaven alone, grace is cheap, and community is irrelevant. It's not surprising that we get the rest of the story wrong if we have a warped understanding of the final picture. It is not surprising that we fail to understand our fundamental identities if we have such a thin understanding of who we are ultimately intended to be.

The final snapshot of eternity provided in Scripture is something altogether different from this individualized and sterile misunderstanding of heaven. The final scene is a wedding: Jesus Christ greets his bride—not one individual but the collective people of God. It is a communal party encompassing every ethnicity across every generation. This is the true culmination of God's story with us that began at creation. In this final picture, we witness the angels triumphantly singing,

> "Let us rejoice and exult
>   and give him the glory,
> for the marriage of the Lamb has come,
>   and his Bride has made herself ready;
> it was granted her to clothe herself
>   with fine linen, bright and pure"—

for the fine linen is the righteous deeds of the saints. (Rev. 19:7–8)

We are holy and beautiful, clothed with the righteousness given by the outworking of Christ's grace in us. Amazingly, God has made us one and made us pure. There is a grain of truth in our intuition that someone else can "complete us." But in the Spirit, we are completed by the bride of Christ, not by our spouse. The Spirit of God has made us to be united with the people of God (the bride) and the Son of God (the Groom). Because of this miraculous work, we will be complete on that final day, lacking nothing.

We are completed by the bride of Christ, not by our spouse.

As the story continues, we see that God's dwelling place is with his bride: "I heard a loud voice from the throne saying, 'Behold, the dwelling place of God is with man. He will dwell with them, and they will be his people, and God himself will be with them as their God'" (21:3). The story of God and his people, from the beginning, has been the story of God dwelling with his people. God walked with Adam and Eve in the garden and will one day dwell with us face-to-face. Not only were we created to be in community with others, but we were all created to be together with God.

Later in Revelation 21, we are shown another scene involving the bride. "Then came one of the seven angels . . . and spoke to me, saying, 'Come, I will show you the Bride, the wife of the Lamb.' And he carried me away in the Spirit to a great, high mountain, and showed me the holy city Jerusalem coming down out of heaven from God, having the glory of God, its radiance like a most rare jewel, like a jasper, clear as crystal" (vv. 9–11). The beautiful city full of God's people is the bride. Together, as a community of believers, we are beautiful and pure and valuable beyond compare.

As the bride joins the Spirit of God, John calls out the hope of salvation to all who will hear: "The Spirit and the Bride say, 'Come.' And let the one who hears say, 'Come.' And let the one who is thirsty come" (22:17). The bride proclaims an open-ended invitation to salvation—an invitation to be part of her.

When we consider our salvation as something between just us and Jesus, we have truncated God's story—we're missing the collective bride. And when we place our ultimate value in the hands of our spouse, we have made what is intended to be a shadow into the object. What a dangerous place to be when we trust a shadow to support us and hold our spiritual lives up.

The good news is that the picture of the marriage of the bride and the Groom (Jesus) is the true ending of God's story! How does this transform our understanding of Christianity and our identity? What does it mean that this eternal wedding, rather than our earthly wedding, shapes our identity?

We Are the Bride

Together, Christians are the bride of Christ. We are his bride, not individually but collectively. Christ did not come to earth merely to rescue individual sinners but to redeem his bride.

This means that other believers are essential to our faith. It means that we are not fully who we were intended to be on our own. It also means that we are loved. We are chosen. We are sanctified. The fact that we are the bride means that Christ invites us into an eternal, intimate relationship with him forever. He not only saves us from the consequences of our sin, but he redeems us to be with him forever.

Our identity as the bride of Christ is so foundational that the principles for marriage on this earth derive from it. Let's look at how Paul talks about our identity as a bride in his letter to the church at Ephesus. He starts with cosmic truths about who God is and who we are, then digs into the nitty-gritty of life.

As he nears the end of his letter, Paul addresses the application of the gospel to husbands and wives. He begins with words for wives, then moves on to husbands. Paul's admonition to husbands is grounded in Christ's love for the church:

Husbands, love your wives, as Christ loved the church and gave himself up for her, that he might sanctify her, having cleansed her by the washing of water with the word, so that he might present the church to himself in splendor, without spot or wrinkle or any such thing, that she might be holy and without blemish. In the same way husbands should love their wives as their own bodies. . . . "Therefore a man shall leave his father and mother and hold fast to his wife, and the two shall become one flesh." This mystery is profound, and I am saying that it refers to Christ and the church. (Eph. 5:25–28, 31–32)

Who is the husband called to emulate? Jesus himself. How did Jesus love his bride, the church? He "gave himself up for her." And for what purpose? "That he might sanctify her." The Son of God, the second person of the eternal triune God, came as God-in-flesh for his bride and gave himself up to death for the sake of her holiness. He was the first groom.

Paul then turns to a well-worn passage from the second chapter of the Bible. He quotes from Genesis 2:24: "Therefore a man shall leave his father and mother and hold fast to his wife, and the two shall become one flesh." You can almost see Paul look up from writing his letter, exhale, and raise his hands in amazement, saying, "This mystery is profound!" Think about this: one of the finest rabbis of the first century admits that this little phrase in the second chapter of the Bible always made him marvel. It is a mystery.

If that passage is a mystery to Paul, it deserves a deeper look from us. Let's look at God's creation of the first woman, Eve. He does so from the rib of Adam:

The LORD God caused a deep sleep to fall upon the man, and while he slept took one of his ribs and closed up its place with flesh. And the rib that the LORD God had taken from the man he made into a woman and brought her to the man. Then the man said,

"This at last is bone of my bones
and flesh of my flesh;
she shall be called Woman,
because she was taken out of Man."

Therefore a man shall leave his father and his mother and hold fast to his wife, and they shall become one flesh. (Gen. 2:21–24)

Perhaps this passage is so familiar to you that you miss why Paul was so perplexed. He wonders, "What could Moses have been up to when he wrote those concluding words?" Adam, after all, had no parents to leave when he became one flesh with Eve.

And what is the deal with that odd phrase about a *man* leaving his mother and—take note—his father?

In antiquity, it was the woman who would have left her parents to marry her husband and join his family, usually living in the same compound or home as her in-laws. The man didn't leave his father and mother physically, and Moses would have known this. Yet he insists that in marriage it isn't just the woman who leaves her parents. It is the man as well. Marriage, Moses insists, is the foundational relational building block. In no other relationship do two become one. Why is that? And what's the deal with the emphasis on the man leaving his parents?

In movies, those little hidden treats the director hides for uberfans are called "Easter eggs." For instance, Alfred Hitchcock makes a brief cameo in each of his films; it's him winking, saying, "Did you see me?" Harrison Ford, as a nod to his fans, holds an artifact in *Raiders of the Lost Ark* that includes hieroglyphs of C-3PO and R2-D2. Speaking of *Star Wars*, in episode 1, E.T. and his family make a fleeting appearance. And how about Rapunzel showing up in the coronation scene in *Frozen*? All Easter eggs!

Yet each of them is dwarfed by the mother of all Easter eggs in Genesis 2. After Paul became a follower of Jesus, he understood how the puzzle pieces fit together. He saw that, from the very beginning, God had given us marriage as a holy picture of his great love for us. Moses's words are a pointer to the ultimate bridegroom, God himself.

Before sin was even in the world, God designed a relationship that would serve as a picture of his great rescue plan: one day the Son of God would come for his bride. "Therefore a man shall leave his father and his mother and hold fast to his wife, and they shall become one flesh." The "therefore" of Genesis 2:24 points us ultimately to the work of God himself: Jesus leaves his Father and comes for his bride.

Jesus the Groom

On various occasions Jesus refers to himself as the bridegroom and his people as his bride. When asked why his disciples don't fast like the Pharisees, Jesus defends them: "Can the wedding guests mourn as long as the bridegroom is with them? The days will come when the bridegroom is taken away from them, and then they will fast" (Matt. 9:15). When we fast (and we should fast), it should point to our yearning for our groom.

Later, Jesus explains what it looks like to live as the church in this world. We are to be marked by diligent expectation of our groom. He shares this parable as a picture of how we are to live in a state of holy preparedness:

> The kingdom of heaven will be like ten virgins who took
> their lamps and went to meet the bridegroom. . . . As the
> bridegroom was delayed, they all became drowsy and slept.

But at midnight there was a cry, "Here is the bridegroom! Come out to meet him." Then all those virgins rose and trimmed their lamps. (Matt. 25:1, 5–7)

If Christ is our groom, then we must be those who wait together for his coming. We are those who wait for the groom who came to betroth himself to us two thousand years ago and will come again on that final, glorious wedding day. When our eyes are set upon Christ for our completion, our expectation for happiness in this life changes. We don't expect our human spouse to make us happy, or our job, or children, or anything else. We don't expect our joy to be complete until we, Christ's bride, are wed to him on that final day.

Today we are in the period of betrothal. The bride doesn't expect her joy to be complete while she is sending out wedding invitations or working extra shifts to pay for the wedding. She expects her joy to overflow when she celebrates face-to-face with her groom on their wedding day.

One of the dangers of seeking our primary identity in our earthly marriages and not our eternal marriage is that it dampens our anticipation for eternity. If we believe we are "completed" by our spouse, we feel like our deep spiritual need for completion should be met. We also turn inward, neglecting relationships beyond our relationship with our spouse. It is probably not an accident that the period of life where individuals withdraw from church the most is in their twenties, when they are often discovering romantic partners.

Seeing the Bride as Lovely

Let's make sure we understand this picture correctly. The bride isn't you or me individually. It is Christ's church collectively. Paul says, "We, though many, are one body in Christ, and individually members one of another" (Rom. 12:5). And Christ came for us. He thinks we are beautiful. The grand culmination of history will be our entrance on that glorious day, the wedding day of Christ and his bride.

As Paul reminds us in Ephesians 5, on that day we will be spectacular. You've seen glimpses of this in the radiant faces of brides on this earth, haven't you? Smiles so wide that cheeks ache at night's end. Eyes that sparkle with so much joy they seem like they were photoshopped. Christ is making us even more beautiful. Tim and Kathy Keller reflect, "When Jesus looked down from the cross, he didn't think 'I am giving myself to you because you are so attractive to me.' No, he was in agony, and he looked down at us—denying him, abandoning him, and betraying him—and in the greatest act of love in history, he *stayed*. He said, 'Father, forgive them, they don't know what they are doing.' He loved us, not because we were lovely to him, but to make us lovely."[3]

And Christ does make believers lovely. In Isaiah 61:10 we see a reflection of what we, as his dazzling bride, will look like: "He has clothed me with the garments of salvation; he has covered me with the robe of righteousness." We are being made pure in character through his sanctification and are already, in Christ, perfectly justified in heaven's court. We love praying Paul's promise in Philippians 1:6 over couples at their wedding: "I am sure of this, that he who began a good work in you will bring it to completion at the day of Jesus Christ."

This endeavor to make us lovely is, by its very nature, a corporate endeavor. Our destiny is connected to the body to which we belong. Unfortunately, the community of believers has gotten a bad rap. To some extent, there's good reason for that. However, Scripture is clear that it's imperative for believers to be with other believers consistently in a loving, reciprocal relationship that encourages and convicts. There are some important takeaways when we consider this. We'll do so in the next few sections.

You Can't Hate the Church

Seventy-two percent of Americans call themselves Christian, but one-third of those identify as "not religious at all," and many more are disconnected from the bride of Christ.[4] In other words, nearly a quarter of the population considers themselves simultaneously Christian and not religious.

It makes sense. Church doesn't always seem to have a daily importance. And really, why commit yourself to an institution with such a checkered reputation? Can't we live out our lives as Christians on our own? Isn't Christianity about a relationship, not religion? Can't I be who God wants me to be without becoming one of those "church people"?

Scripture is clear: Just like we can't love our spouse and not hang out with them, we can't love Christ and disengage from his people. Christ gave his life for the church. Our love is connected to the body we are a part of.

Many American Christians have this inversed. They love their wives (or husbands) well, but they have no use for Christ's bride. As a pastor and a counselor, we have met with many who have told us the same story: "I've been so burned by the church. I've been there and done that. I am not going back." Our hearts ache as we listen to their hurt and doubly ache when we see how compensating for that pain has turned into bitterness and, eventually, a hardness of heart. When our hearts harden, we turn away from Jesus and his mission to reconcile with his bride. There are reasons to leave an unhealthy church: false teaching, divisiveness, and ungodliness being three Paul mentions (1 Tim. 6:3–5). Christ mourns these abuses, but he also invites us back into community, risking the vulnerability that it entails. Leaving a local church for legitimate reasons ought not have us disconnecting from a committed body of believers altogether. Jesus doesn't give up on his church, and neither should we. The bride of Christ is made up of broken people who, like us, need forgiveness. There may be times when, because of abuse or heresy, we need to break fellowship with a local church, but such a decision needs to be carried out in a God-honoring way, and we then must do the hard work of stepping into community with another church.

Jesus doesn't give up on his church, and neither should we.

Does your Christian community have to be in a building with a steeple? Perhaps not. The pandemic revealed that online small group meetings can't be avoided sometimes. And it's shown that the bride—that is, the universal church—needs to be flexible in some areas. But Scripture is clear that we should not give up meeting together for the purpose of accountability and encouragement (Heb. 10:25), whether there's a building with a steeple or not.

Is the bride a literal church building? No.

Are the basic things such as corporate worship, communion, and the preaching of God's Word that ought to happen inside those buildings required? Yes.

And the fact remains that for most believers in the West, the local church is where we are most likely to find the bride functioning. Let's also be honest and admit that it's difficult to build real relationships without some form of face-to-face contact. Research proves that "face-to-face interactions have benefits that virtual communication may lack."[5]

To the degree we cut the bride out of our life, we reject Jesus and cut him off. Imagine that your best friend's husband is the last person you would befriend. When you go out on double dates, he always lets you pick up the tab, he eats with his mouth open, and he is twice as loud as necessary. But your best friend loves her husband and sees him as charming and quirky. Your dislike of him will significantly impact your relationship with her, won't it? You know that if you force her to choose between the two of you, she is going to stick with her husband, and rightly so. You cannot love your best friend and hate her husband. We cannot love Christ and hate the church. Christ delights in his bride, quirks and all. We don't get to keep him and kick her to the curb. She is the apple of his eye.

We cannot love Christ and hate the church.

Pew Research Center recently released a survey detailing why Americans do and do not attend church.[6] While 73 percent of Americans identify as being Christian, another survey reveals that the proportion of Americans who report going to church weekly is only around 35 percent.[7] Best estimates for our own city, Tucson, indicate that less than 10 percent of the population attend church regularly,[8] and only around 3 percent attend church on any given Sunday.[9]

That means that over half of professing Christians nationally probably have no supportive body of believers.

We shouldn't be surprised about church attendance when Christian belief has become so diluted. Studies have demonstrated that American Christians have lackluster engagement with the Bible and a weak understanding of the Bible and theology. For instance, only 51 percent of Americans know that Jesus delivered the Sermon on the Mount;[10] 59 percent believe the Holy Spirit is a force, not a personal Being; and 52 percent believe Jesus was a great teacher but not God.[11] A thin Christianity that is understood as agreeing with a few minimal theological propositions (I believe in God, I believe in Jesus, I believe I'm a sinner, and if I believe in Jesus, he will save me) is a Christianity without a *need* for community—a brideless Christianity. No community is needed to believe these propositions.

If Christianity is reduced to a mere set of beliefs and not entrusting ourselves to our Groom, whose purposes for us are entwined with his purposes for his bride, then our trajectory will naturally be individualistic. But if we understand the greater story of the Bible, a tale of God's redemption of a people, then we will see meeting together with the church not as an add-on but at the core of God's purposes.

No Church, No Identity

When God's people live outside of the church, we are not fully who God intended us to be. We are made for community (Gen. 1–2; John 13:34–35). We're each given gifts to support the bride. When we cut ourselves off from the church, we cut ourselves off from God's purposes for us. For us to be most fully who we are, we must be part of God's community, not just in theory but also in practice. We are complete when we serve with our gifts and receive gifts from others. We are complete when we ask for forgiveness. We are complete when we forgive one another. We are complete when we are united with those who are very different from us. We are complete when we love those who are hard to love.

This begins first with committing to a community of believers who, as I stated earlier, meet regularly and are willing and able to encourage us and give us accountability. Our commitment then builds into deeper engagement. Most believers don't belong to a steadfast group of believers, much less understand their identity as connected to the church in a meaningful way. Why is that? In a recent survey, those reasons were expressed in the following ways.[12]

"I Practice My Faith in Other Ways"

This statement reflects the largest group, 37 percent, of those who don't attend church. Practicing our faith outside of Sunday morning is wonderful, of course. It isn't meant to be sustained by corporate worship alone; it is to be expressed daily and through various means. However, let's be blunt: there is no space in the New Testament for authentic Christianity expressed outside of the context of a group of believers who meet regularly together—and that group is most typically found in a local church.

Twenty-two of the twenty-seven New Testament books are letters, and of those, twenty-one are likely written to churches or leaders of churches.[13] Paul writes "to the church of God that is in Corinth" (1 Cor. 1:2), "To the churches of Galatia" (Gal. 1:2), and "To the church of the Thessalonians in God the Father and the Lord Jesus Christ" (1 Thess. 1:1). John writes "to the seven churches that are in Asia" (Rev. 1:4). Even when not referencing specific churches, the letters are clearly written for the church. For instance, Paul writes "to all the saints in Christ Jesus who are at Philippi, with the overseers and deacons" (Phil. 1:1).

But wait—the early church was different from today's church. They met in homes, not in buildings, right?

While undeniable cultural changes have happened, churches are not different in essence. They are still the local gathering of God's people, brought together to proclaim the gospel, worship the risen Jesus, and serve one another. Local churches were led by elders, with deacons leading the ministry of the church. Just as today, teaching elders were normally paid for their ministry (2 Thess. 3:7–10; 1 Cor. 9:9–14; Phil. 4:16–19). These gatherings met in the atrium area of first-century Roman villas, which seated between fifty and one hundred and fifty people[14] and were often beautifully decorated with wall paintings and even baptisteries.[15] Interestingly, the median church today is sixty-five people.[16]

From the resurrection of Jesus onward, the New Testament is the story of God's work of salvation in and through the gathering of believers. Why is that? Because this is the way God designed it. God's design reflects his character. Our three-in-one God is a God in whom perfect community exists. Part of being created in the image of God is being created to exist in community. God's work has always been done through a people and is leading toward the union of a diverse people.[17] Do you long for unity in a divided culture? The church, as expressed most reliably in the local congregation, is intended to be a beacon of unity and completeness.

No Real Reason

The second-largest group of non-church-going believers claim, "No reason." Are you letting the niggling realities of life, such as sleeping in, watching football, exercise, and so on prevent you from living in the fullness of God's call on your life? God intends, in his power, to sanctify you through his bride. God longs to bless you through his people. We turn away from God's invitation for us when we pull away from the church.

It's the Church's Fault

The next three reasons all point the finger at the local church: "I haven't found a church I like" (23 percent); "I don't like the sermons" (18 percent); and "I don't feel welcome" (14 percent).

Any person who has spent any time at church has been failed by a church. Churches are filled with humans who can fail in all sorts of ways. We can be lousy at welcoming newcomers, choosing instead to catch up with our friends. We can play good music badly or bad music well. And John admits he has preached more than a few sermons he wishes he could redo because they were boring, awkward, or unclear.

> **Churches are filled with humans who can fail in all sorts of ways.**

We naturally align with those who like the same things we like, do the same things we do, are of the same age, ethnicity, education, and income. But the church draws together people who often have no reason other than Jesus to be together. In the early church gatherings, slaves and free, rich and poor, Jews and Gentiles alike were all drawn together. Our allegiance to Christ and our equality at the foot of the cross builds a diverse community. The love of Christ expels our fear of difference. As the apostle John says, "We love because he first loved us" (1 John 4:19). The biblical scholar D. A. Carson once noted that "the church itself is not made up of natural 'friends.' It is made up of natural enemies . . . who love one another for Jesus' sake."[18]

This view is simultaneously discouraging and encouraging. The Christian community shouldn't naturally click. Getting along should be hard. We come from different backgrounds with different ethnicities, different political allegiances, and different socioeconomic statuses. We are not naturally friends. To forge friendships in this group of misfits is a true work of God. We shouldn't expect friendship to come easily, and we shouldn't be surprised when we are let down. Instead, we ought to commit ourselves to do everything in our power to step into relationships with those who aren't naturally our friends.

Pastor Dietrich Bonhoeffer has a rebuke for when the sins of other Christians loom large to us. He says,

> If my sin appears to me to be in any way smaller or less reprehensible in comparison with the sins of others, then I am not yet recognizing my sin at all. . . . Christian love will find any number of excuses for the sins of others; only for my sin is there no excuse whatsoever. . . . Those who would serve others in the community must descend all the way down to this depth of humility. How could I possibly serve other persons in unfeigned humility if their sins appear to me to be seriously worse than my own?[19]

In other words, when we are discouraged and frustrated by our local church, are we appropriately considering our own failings? Or are we so focused on the failings of others that we cannot see our own sin? This is not to say that we ignore sin or cover up the sin of church leaders, but when it comes to shortcomings, do we magnify others' weaknesses while minimizing our own? Jesus once humorously brought this point home by speaking of someone intent on taking the speck out of his brother's eye while having a whole plank of wood sticking out of his own eye (Matt. 7:4). It is easier to see another's speck than our plank. Once our plank is out, we may then address the other's speck.

Your Identity and Christ's Bride

Of course, community cannot and does not replace the need for Christ's work in our hearts. Christ's invitation into community isn't an invitation into codependence. The gift of our relationship with Christ is that we do know him individually. We do experience the transforming work of the Holy Spirit personally. And we have a relationship with God directly as sons, priests, saints, sheep, and more. When we understand the interplay of these identities, both individually and corporately, we can experience the fullness of what God has for us.

So give the church a chance. And when she fails you, give her another chance. You might have hit her on a bad day. First, find a solid church. You can research a church on its website and watch worship services online before you visit, thereby ensuring its fidelity to the gospel and getting a sense of their engagement in the mission of Christ.

Then, once you commit, really commit. Commit to a local gathering of God's people that God has called you to through thick and thin.

We can't put this too strongly: you really don't have an option. Your identity is bound with Christ's bride. Our future redemption is with God's people. We are fully who God intended us to be as we stoop to wash the feet of Christ's people, joyfully serve, humbly repent, and graciously forgive. In our unity we reflect the love of Christ to a world scarred with division.

> ## In our unity we reflect the love of Christ to a world scarred with division.

Our hearts are saddened as we consider those who once faithfully attended, even served and led, who no longer gather with other believers in any meaningful way. They have cut themselves off from the final scene of God's rescue. They are nowhere to be seen in the final frame of the great story. They have abandoned being God's bride. The point isn't that we earn salvation by going to church; rather, a decision to cut oneself off from Christian community ought to give one pause about whether one is abiding in Christ.

I don't know how to put this more graciously. If you are not invested in your fellow believers, you are missing out on a critical part of how God has made you. In fact, you are disobeying him.

Outside the Church, No One Is Saved

On the night before he was crucified, Jesus drilled into his disciples how important it was to love each other. At the Last Supper, Jesus told his disciples that their discipleship would be marked first by their love for one another: "By this all people will know that you are my disciples, if you have love for one another" (John 13:35). Then later that night, Jesus tells them their unity is of utmost importance. He prays to his Father that his disciples "may become perfectly one, so that the world may know that you sent me and loved them even as you loved me" (17:23).

The early Christians understood the importance of unity in the church. Irenaeus, who lived in the second century, said that the church "is the entrance to life; all others are thieves and robbers."[20] Origen, during the third century, said, "Let no one deceive himself. Outside this house, that is, outside the Church, no one is saved."[21] And Saint Cyprian of Carthage, who lived in the third century, stated, "There is no salvation out of the Church."[22] They understood that Christ's redemptive purposes were bound to the collective witness of his people.

Commitment to a group of believers is not meant to be rote. It's not checking a box. It's intentional and relational. Our love for one another is Christ's primary tool for evangelism. We are intended to have rich and meaningful community in the church, to practice radical hospitality toward one another, and to selflessly serve one another. In fact, in chapter 9 we will consider how God has given you specific gifts to serve the church.[23]

Friends, we need the church. We can't have the end of God's story without her. In our participation with the bride, as we love, forgive, reconcile, serve, and gather, something supernatural is happening. God is on a mission through his bride. We can't experience love as God intended without her. We can't show Christ's love to the world as he intended without her. In all the church's messiness and in all her faltering, we still need her. We need her because God's kingdom is bigger than us individually. We need her because God's work on earth is through his bride, the church. We need her because, like the church, we also are messy, and we also falter. And we need God's bride to call us back to our Groom.

PRAYER

Jesus, my Bridegroom, forgive me for being unfaithful to your bride. Forgive me for the ways I have looked to my spouse to provide what only you can. I've chosen my rags over the pure garments of salvation you have offered. I've chosen myself over you. I've considered my identity merely as an individual and rarely as part of your bride. Please do your work of sanctification in me. Give me a longing for righteousness and purity. Give me a devotion to your bride, the church. Show me the ways I need her. Give me eyes to see the ending of the story, the marriage of the groom and his bride. Help me to live in anticipation of and preparation for that day. Amen.

Parenthood
Finding Belonging as an Adopted Son

~

Having children just puts the whole world into perspective. Everything else just disappears.
—Kate Winslet

*I am a pilgrim and a stranger on the earth,
but I am not an orphan.*
—Vance Havner

*Adoption . . . is an act of transfer from an alien family
into the family of God himself. This is surely the apex of
grace and privilege.*
—John Murray

ANGEL

I SAT ACROSS FROM OLIVIA. Her hands and her voice shook. "All my life I wanted to be a mom. I was so excited to get married, mostly because then I could finally be a mom. Six months after our wedding day we got pregnant. We were so excited! We began picking out names and preparing the nursery. At four months, I miscarried. I was so angry with God. How could he let this happen? Isn't this what he made me for?"

She began to cry. I let the quietness sit in the room. Olivia continued, "A year passed and we got pregnant again. We were excited but afraid. I kept waiting to lose the baby and at four months, I miscarried again. I yelled at God, 'If you love me, why are you allowing this to happen?' I was so bitter."

Her tears continued to flow. "I miscarried a third time, and then I gave up on God's goodness. I guess I made a vow to God that I wouldn't trust him again. My husband and I started looking into adoption, and in the middle of the process we got pregnant again. I resolved I wouldn't let him die. I was meticulous with exercise, health, and rest. I made sure nothing would get in the way of my baby's life. God failed me three times in pregnancy. I was going to take control of this pregnancy. Months passed and my precious baby was born. I finally had what I wanted all those years: I was a mom."

"What does it mean to you that you are a mom?" I asked.

"It is my job to protect. It is my responsibility to keep my son safe. He is my everything. If he's happy, then I am happy. Everyone jokes that our son is the prince. But he is my purpose."

I sit across from another counselee. It's our first session. "Our youngest daughter heads to college in six months. More and more she is demanding freedom. She tells me I am a helicopter mom and that I need to release her. But I don't know how to let go. I've only ever wanted to be a mom. Every decision I make is filtered by being her mom. Who am I when she leaves?"

Another client, and a heaviness fills the room. "Tell me about your marriage," I ask.

"My husband hates me. I gave myself to my kids before I gave to my husband. He got the leftovers. He resents me now. I feel hopeless. I've lost control of my life. Who am I if I am not a mom?"

Not all will experience the challenge and the gift of being a parent, but many long to hold a child and be called "Mommy" or "Daddy." Some ache at a child's death. And others are disappointed by infertility. Whatever your circumstance, it can be easy to place one's identity in the ideal of being a parent.

For those who are parents, you'll relate—you never forget the first moment you hold your child. Our firstborn, Camille, came into the world with big, bright blue eyes. She couldn't hold her shining eyes open wide enough. There was so much to take in and absorb. Today Camille lives in fifth gear, with insatiable curiosity and relentless energy. Our secondborn, Soren, had to be coaxed to open his eyes. He exited the womb like a curled panda bear. Mellow and easygoing, Soren gets along with everyone and is rarely ruffled.

One year ago, Camille graduated from high school. Our son is less than a year away from his graduation. We look at the years we've been blessed to actively shepherd their hearts as some of the most life-giving years of our lives. We couldn't be more thankful for our kids. They are two of the greatest gifts we have ever been given.

Is there any role more challenging or rewarding than that of a parent?

As parents we pour out our hearts, our time, and our energy for our kids. We grieve when they are sad, and we glow when they are filled with joy. We are heartbroken when they are picked on at school, and we are so proud when they master a challenging subject.

In short, our hearts are tethered to our children's hearts in ways that are hard to explain if you aren't a parent. That heart tie can lure us to think that being a mom or dad is part of our identity, and even a healthy part. After all, what could be dangerous about identifying yourself as a mom or a dad?

But our true identity was never intended to be as mom or dad. Even when they are minors, our children do not belong to us; they belong to God. Tethering our children to ourselves creates codependency.

We cannot siphon our identity from our children's well-being. Such codependency puts our souls in danger. If our success and worth are found in how well our children behave or in what they achieve, we are in spiritual danger. When we can only experience joy if our children are happy, it exposes the fact that our children have become idols for us. And since, with any idol, our purpose is found in appeasing it, we parent with the goal of having our children be happy with us and the world around them. We seek to manage our children—but, ironically, we are controlled by them. In this codependent relationship, we believe our children's behavior is a direct reflection of us. With our reputation at stake, we try to manipulate our children to behave in a manner that is not in their best interest but ours.

When we can only experience joy if our children are happy, it exposes the fact that our children have become idols for us.

The truth is, our godliness as parents does not guarantee our children's godliness (and, praise God, our sin doesn't guarantee our children's sin). It is a dangerous thing to anchor our identity to the choices our children will make in life. Many parents have been wrecked emotionally and spiritually by their children's failures. And many have had their egos balloon with their children's successes.

When your child throws a tantrum, your worth is not diminished. When your child earns straight As, your worth is not increased.

As strong as our bonds to our children are, we are not intended to be one with them. Adult children should have the freedom to establish their own lives and follow the Lord's leading, even if it takes them halfway around the world. And if our children marry, they ought to be united to their spouses. The only one-flesh union on this earth is not between parent and child; it is between husband and wife. And, as we have already explored in chapter 6, even that isn't part of our identity. Our children's choices, their marriages, and even the possibility of their deaths remind us that being Mom or Dad is a role we're to steward as unto the Lord—a very important role, yes, but it is not an identity.

That can feel like bad news. What else are we supposed to do? For some, there are few things more life giving than our relationships with our children and the gift of caring for them as their parents. For others, parenting is one of the few things we think we've gotten mostly right. Why would God take that identity away from us?

Hang with me here. There is good news. It isn't that God is taking the identity of parent away from us; rather, he's giving us new eyes to see that parenting is a role to steward because he is the Great Parent. Our identity is grounded in our relationship with our heavenly Father, not in our relationship with our children. This means our identity is found in our status as a child of God, not as a mom or dad.

The implications of God's adopting us are transformative—and permanent. The role of parent can change at any time, but our adoption as sons* of God cannot be removed by any person or circumstance.

---

* We understand the word *sons* may sound sexist to some. But in its biblical context, it has an important significance that transcends gender. I'll explain in a bit. For now, we promise you that sonship doesn't exclude women any more than being Christ's bride excludes men.

Exchanging your identity as a parent for your true identity as a son of God gives you permission to yield control and fear to God and receive, in return, his peace and promises of faithfulness toward you and your children. It gives you permission to surrender your children, knowing your limitations in this role as parent, to their perfect, never-changing, constant advocate, their loving Abba Father, who hears their every breath and has established each of their steps. When we entrust our kids to the Lord, we parent in grace and truth, not in bondage and exhaustion.

But what does it mean, practically, that God is our heavenly Father?

Abba's Adopted

Our adoption began with God's choosing us despite ourselves. In our natural state, we were enemies of God and slaves to the flesh. Yet, even while we resisted, God called us into his family. Paul says we "have received the Spirit of adoption as sons, by whom we cry, 'Abba! Father!'" (Rom. 8:15).

Abba is the Aramaic word for "father." (Aramaic was the colloquial language of Jews of that time.) We would say "dad" or "daddy." Jesus calls the first person of the Trinity *Abba*.

Maybe calling God Abba doesn't feel like good news to you. Maybe you had, or have, an earthly dad who has wounded you. Our hearts hurt for you. It is not as it should have been. We pray you can know that pain is real for Jesus too. He went to the cross for you, for your pain. His blood permits you to not be defined by the core messages you heard from your earthly father.

Perhaps you heard the message that you aren't enough or aren't worth anyone's effort and time. Jesus spoke a new message to you at the cross. He not only saw each wounding message of your childhood, but he went to great lengths to feel it and die on your behalf. The intentionality of his blood spilled for you is a message of tremendous worth. You are invited to hear Jesus whisper over you as he bleeds, "You are so worth it. You are enough. You are my joy and delight." He knows you well, knows your pain—and he welcomes you to know God as Abba: the true Father whom God intended you to experience. As pastor Louie Giglio says, "God is not simply the reflection of your earthly dad. God is the perfection of your earthly dad."[1]

But before you can settle into your role as adopted child, you might need to know exactly what a perfect father looks like.

The Forgiven Enemy Son

Eric Geiger, in his book *Identity*, recalls the story of Mephibosheth as a pointer to our identity as adopted sons of God.[2] Unless you maxed out your gold stars in Sunday school as a kid, or you have read your Bible cover to cover a few times, I know what you're thinking right now: *Mephibo-who?*

The story of Mephibosheth comes at the beginning of the reign of King David. Not only was David the former shepherd boy who took on the giant with a slingshot, he was also the writer of many of the psalms and was called a man after God's own heart. Before David, Saul was king, and he wasn't too keen on David. In fact, he hunted the younger man for years, maybe even decades. But then came a battle with the dreaded Amalekites. Israel was losing, and Saul, sensing defeat, committed suicide.

If you've seen any movie about ancient kingdoms, you don't need me to tell you about the next step for David. Whenever a new line took the throne, the king eliminated the old line. There could be no rival claimants to the throne.

Mephibosheth was the one final heir left in Saul's line, his grandson, crippled in both feet. For years he lives in obscurity, likely hoping he will continue to avoid the king's attention. But one day, Mephibosheth is summoned to the king's chambers; he knows exactly what awaits him.

Picture it. He comes in, shaking in fear, and falls to his face before David. "I am your servant," he says.

But David has no intention of harming Mephibosheth. Rather, he is about to exalt the young man. "Don't worry, I'm your friend," he tells Mephibosheth. "I won't kill you. In fact, I'll give you your grandfather's land, and you can come have dinner with me anytime" (2 Sam. 9:7, paraphrase mine).

Mephibosheth can hardly believe what he hears. "What is your servant, that you should show regard for a dead dog such as I?" (v. 8).

Doomed to death, this crippled man has instead just been adopted as a son into the king's family.

Here's the deal: You and I are Mephibosheth. Enemies of God headed toward damnation, we have instead been invited into the Father's house with honor. Once crippled by our sin, we are now healed by the work of the Son of God and chosen as heirs to the Father's vast kingdom. In Christ, this is true for your believing children as well. Knowing we stand equal as adopted sons alongside our children empowers us to shepherd their hearts and minds under our Great Shepherd and releases us from any false power of identity as their parents.

From enemies to sons. From dead to alive. From thieves and robbers to children in our Father's house. Isn't that incredible? We love the way Mark Buchanan reflects on this truth: "This is the love of God: an alchemy that can turn enemies into children."[3] Like the frog in the fairy tale of the princess's kiss, we have been transformed into princes.

From enemies to sons. From dead to alive. From thieves and robbers to children in our Father's house. Isn't that incredible?

When our children passed their driver's tests, they received a driver's license, documentation that allows them to legally operate a vehicle. By mailing those licenses, the state of Arizona was declaring it would now treat our children differently. With the licenses came both opportunity and responsibility. Similarly, when God chose us as his sons, we received much more than just a change of status. We do not merely move from being guilty to being acquitted; we are brought into God's family and treated as sons.

Let's stop for just a minute and ask a question we know might be rattling around in your head: All of us, male and female alike . . . *sons*?

In short, yes. Sons. That narrow word might give you pause. You might be expecting us to make our language gender neutral, "sons and daughters." But here is the strange thing: Women are never referred to as "daughters of God" in the Bible. That's rather odd, given how often the phrase is used in Christian circles. An Amazon search for "daughter of God" nets over one thousand books. In the Bible, however, the seemingly exclusive phrase "sons of God" is used for men and women alike.

What gives? Is this a linguistic fluke? Hidden misogyny? Is the lack of inclusion of daughters a patriarchal blind spot in the Bible we ought to rectify? On the contrary: the use of "sons of God" is a radical move by the authors of Scripture that raises the status of women.

Allow me to explain: In the ancient world, Israel included for the most part,[4] only sons received the family inheritance. Daughters received no inheritance. They were dependent on their husband or the care of their family. If the biblical authors referred to men and women as "sons and daughters of God," then their readers might have mistakenly presumed that only men received a spiritual inheritance from God.[5]

By referring to all the children of God as "sons of God," the biblical authors are saying something profound: men and women are equal recipients of the inheritance of the Father. Isn't it amazing how the Bible undermines our cultural expectations?

There are no second-class citizens, no minor roles to play. Women are equal heirs to the kingdom. So when we talk about the benefits of adoption, all believers benefit equally.

Being a son of God guarantees the following:

- the Father's inheritance
- the Father's attention
- the Father's care
- the Father's family

The Father's Inheritance

The most important inheritance we are promised is Christ himself. That means we have access to God.

When we recently visited Washington, DC, for some reason the president didn't put us on his calendar. But we can step into the throne room of the Almighty today. We are guaranteed to be in the triune presence for eternity. We are also guaranteed the blessings of living in a redeemed state. We will live eternally in resurrected bodies. We are guaranteed the blessings of life in the new heavens and new earth. We will work, and it will not be toil. We will experience peace and the physical blessings of life God intended for us. Finally, we are guaranteed the gift of the family of God, who will dwell in peace together.

The Father's Attention

Sonship also promises us the attention of the Father.

In his letter to the Galatians, Paul says:

> I mean that the heir, as long as he is a child, is no different from a slave, though he is the owner of everything, but he is under guardians and managers until the date set by his father. In the same way we also, when we were children,

were enslaved to the elementary principles of the world. But when the fullness of time had come, God sent forth his Son, born of woman, born under the law, to redeem those who were under the law, so that we might receive adoption as sons. And because you are sons, God has sent the Spirit of his Son into our hearts, crying, "Abba! Father!" So you are no longer a slave, but a son, and if a son, then an heir through God. (Gal. 4:1–7)

What an incredible promise: all of us, men and women alike, who were enslaved to the world have been purchased by the price of the Son so we could be adopted as sons of God. And now God invites us who were once estranged from him to lovingly cry out to him, "Dad!" What an invitation! What a reality!

We have the Father's ear. Unlike our earthly fathers, who can be inattentive at times, our heavenly Father is never inattentive. Unlike our earthly fathers, who can be weary of us oversharing or over-asking, our heavenly Father never grows weary. "Call out to me," he invites. Unlike our earthly fathers, who may abuse and take advantage of us, our heavenly Father loves and respects us unconditionally. That is his nature. Our Father truly is our safe place. Can you picture yourself running into his arms? Dropping into his lap?

> **God invites us who were once estranged from him to lovingly cry out to him, "Dad!"**

We can talk to God through prayer because we are the Father's children, and a child never has to apologize when he seeks the attention of his daddy. In fact, a good daddy delights when his child seeks out his attention, when his child asks questions and listens intently for the response. We love the way Paul Miller reflects on this truth. He says, "To learn how to pray is to enter the world of a child, where all things are possible."[6] Does childlikeness characterize your approach to God?

We are God's kids, and he is along for the ride. "Look at me!" we shout, and he smiles in return and says, "Do it again!" Scripture says God delights in us (Ps. 18:19) and that we're his masterpiece (Eph. 2:10). God loves hanging out with his kids and is delighted by our quirks, passions, talents, and abilities. After all, he made us. God issues each of us an invitation to enjoy him while we find joy. God loves that my dad loves the sweetness of milk chocolate. And he loves that I love the sweet bitterness of dark chocolate instead. As we savor, he savors. God wants us to bring him into our joy and our laughter. Now, doesn't that sound like a great way to release a little stress?

The Father's Care

When he writes to the church at Rome, Paul frames our sonship this way:

> All who are led by the Spirit of God are sons of God. For you did not receive the spirit of slavery to fall back into fear, but you have received the Spirit of adoption as sons, by whom we cry, "Abba! Father!" The Spirit himself bears witness with our spirit that we are children of God, and if children, then heirs—heirs of God and fellow heirs with Christ, provided we suffer with him in order that we may also be glorified with him. (Rom. 8:14–17)

Here Paul frames the reality of our adoption through the work of the Spirit. Our adoption as sons means we have no more reason to fear—how can we? The God of the universe is our Dad. What can we possibly be afraid of? God cares for us. As sons of God, we look like our brother, Jesus. Do you know a family that doesn't look alike, but you know they belong together? They have the same sense of humor, the same walk, the same tastes, the same laugh. Christians are like that. We share traits of our brother, Jesus (Heb. 2:11; Rom. 8:29; Mark 3:34). Dietrich Bonhoeffer reminds us, "It is only because he became like us that we can become like him."[7]

If you want to see the character of what God intends us to become, look to Jesus. His life looks like suffering that ends in glory, so we should not be surprised that our own lives are marked by suffering, and we should anticipate the glorious inheritance that has been secured by our brother, Jesus.

Our suffering does not mean God has forgotten us or does not care for us. On the contrary, if we do not suffer, then we probably should be concerned. The author of the book of Hebrews says this shocking statement that flips how so many of us think about times of suffering in our lives:

> "My son, do not regard lightly the discipline of the Lord,
> nor be weary when reproved by him.
> For the Lord disciplines the one he loves,
> and chastises every son whom he receives."
>
> It is for discipline that you have to endure. God is treating you as sons. For what son is there whom his father does not discipline? If you are left without discipline, in which all have participated, then you are illegitimate children and not sons. (12:5–8)

It's hard to overstate just how countercultural that statement is. When we counsel those who are walking through times of suffering, this is often a passage we point to. In a world where some of the loudest proponents of Christianity declare that, in Christianity, you will experience "your best life now," this passage comes like a splash of freezing-cold water across the face. What if your righteousness on the other side of your suffering outweighs your grief? What if your conformity to Christ outshines the darkness? What if your character and the fruit of the Spirit you display amid pain and suffering are the amplifier for God's goodness to those around you? God disciplines his sons because he cares for them.

A loving father does not let his children do whatever they please. A loving father does not leave his children uncorrected. A loving father does not let his children raise themselves. A loving father disciplines. If our Lord, a perfect Father, who disciplines the one he loves, gives us the role of mom or dad, we too have a responsibility in obedience to do the same. To discipline appropriately is to show grace and love. Being a parent is a profound gift and invitation as unto the Lord; it is not an identity in which we clutch control in order to find peace and satisfaction.

But God's care is not merely in his discipline. We all see God's care as he responds to our needs and frees us from the anxieties of life. In Matthew 6:25–26, Jesus says, "I tell you, do not be anxious about your life, what you will eat or what you will drink, nor about your body, what you will put on. Is not life more than food, and the body more than clothing? Look at the birds of the air: they neither sow nor reap nor gather into barns, and yet your heavenly Father feeds them. Are you not of more value than they?"

God cares for you. Do you trust him? God cares for your children. Do you trust him? There is nothing that gives more peace than walking in your heavenly Father's trust.

Just a chapter later, Jesus encourages us to approach God with our requests, knowing he cares for us. In Matthew 7:9–11 he says, "Which one of you, if his son asks him for bread, will give him a stone? Or if he asks for a fish, will give him a serpent? If you then, who are evil, know how to give good gifts to your children, how much more will your Father who is in heaven give good things to those who ask him!"

What requests are you withholding from God? Do you not know that he delights in giving gifts to his children? He has not withheld his own Son from us; will he not give generously to those who ask (Rom. 8:32)?

James 1:17 reminds us, "Every good gift and every perfect gift is from above, coming down from the Father of lights, with whom there is no variation or shadow due to change." And Paul reminds us in Philippians 4:19–20, "My God will supply every need of yours according to his riches in glory in Christ Jesus. To our God and Father be glory forever and ever. Amen."

God loves us enough to steer us in the right direction, but he also delights in giving to us beyond our wildest expectations . . . if only we can hold on to our trust in him.

The Father's Family

The final, glorious truth in our adoption as sons is that we are not singularly adopted. We are adopted alongside a whole family. You are not an only child.

As Westerners, we tend to derive our value from our individual worth. And it's true, God comes after us individually as those who are lost (see Luke 15, which includes the series of Jesus's parables about finding the lost). And yet, we are not rescued merely into an individual relationship with God. We are part of the greatest family in the history of the world.

**We are adopted alongside a whole family.
You are not an only child.**

Can you imagine being a Rockefeller or a Walton or a Kennedy or a Bush or an Obama or a Trump? Can you imagine the access you would have? The family vacations you would take? The restaurants you would frequent? The financial security you would have? A family matters. And God's family is so much better than any family here. Forget measuring your worth by the thousands or millions or billions; our patriarch owns it *all*. God's wealth is poetically described in Psalm 50:10–11:

> Every beast of the forest is mine,
>> the cattle on a thousand hills.
> I know all the birds of the hills,
>> and all that moves in the field is mine.

Did your mom put your name on everything you had when you were little so you didn't lose it at school? If your heavenly Father wrote his name on all his stuff that way, then every couch, every rock, every tree, every gold bar, every dollar bill, every car would have one name on it: "God." We have the richest Daddy who ever was.

And our family is spread out across the globe. Travel to any inhabited place on the planet, and not far away you can find a sibling. Within minutes, you can share stories about your Dad, reflect on family memories, and get excited about the greatest family vacation ever planned that awaits you both.

John has met family members in remote tribal villages in Senegal, in the Atlas mountains of Morocco, in the crowded streets of Upper Egypt. We've traveled together and met spiritual brothers and sisters in Tamil Nadu, India, and in the small town of Valdez, Alaska. We've met family members in Madison Street Jail in downtown Phoenix, in soup kitchens in Trenton, New Jersey, and at a barbeque joint in St. Louis. Stories of our rescue and our Father are shared. Songs are sung together. Hands are held as prayers are lifted. No shared language is needed to interpret squeezed hands, bear hugs, and moist eyes.

Are you enjoying the benefits of your siblings? Those in the early church were often cast out of their families because of their decision to join this emerging group of Christ followers. Those from Jewish families would have been cast out for following a false messiah, being tritheists (worshiping three gods), and subverting the Jewish religious order. Romans who followed Christ would have been cast out of their families for being part of a religious group that was branded as disruptive, traitorous, and even cannibalistic.

It was no small thing for this group of new believers, many of whom had been rejected by their own families, to understand the new family they belonged to. In his book *Destroyer of the gods*,[8] Larry Hurtado argues that one of the reasons the early church grew explosively was because of its radical inclusivity.

In Ephesians 3, Paul describes this surprising family: "This mystery is that the Gentiles are fellow heirs, members of the same body, and partakers of the promise in Christ Jesus through the gospel. . . . For this reason I bow my knees before the Father, from whom every family in heaven and on earth is named, that according to the riches of his glory he may grant you to be strengthened with power through his Spirit in your inner being" (vv. 6, 14–16). Doesn't our lonely and isolated world yearn for this kind of welcome? Christ invites us to be a family to a world in desperate search of one.

We have been given a new family: a family of every ethnicity, all with one true Father. Our true family is the family of God. We have been given a new last name: sons of God. That was a great hope to the first-century believer. It's no less a hope to us. It's a hope to those who come from broken homes. It's a hope to those who come from healthy homes and are tempted to anchor their security in their family of origin.

The church isn't merely a calling to be part of a group or a club or a place of dynamic individual worship. The church is called to be a family. Like any family this side of heaven, our churches will have conflict, but they ought to be places of security and commitment. Places of transparency and grace. Places where kitchen conversations happen, not just foyer conversations. Places where we can confront and be confronted in love.

Praise to the Father for naming us his own. May he bless you, our brothers and sisters, and may he build up his family in local churches in every corner of the globe.

Good news, men: you're sons! Good news, ladies: you're sons! And what a marvelous truth that is. We, men and women alike, are sons of God, purchased from slavery by the blood of the Son of God, Jesus, adopted by the Father and given his full inheritance. That's worth celebrating.

Parenting as Sons

The truth is, our role as parents is a role of stewardship. And when we parent out of our sonship, our parenting transforms. We can shepherd our children's hearts with grace, entrusting them to the only parent worthy of our full trust: our Abba.

Our children have never been ours to control. All control belongs to their heavenly Father, and the sooner we surrender our children to his care, the freer we will be to love and cheer them on for who God has made them to be, not for who we expect or want them to be. Their Abba has known them from eternity, he has loved them from the womb, and he holds their future in his unfailing hands. When we rest in our Father's love for our kids, we are free to love them without putting them on a pedestal or parenting out of fear.

If we parent from a false identity, we'll eventually suffocate our kids, and we may lose the very relationships we fought so hard to hold on to. But when we step into our parental role out of sonship, we can point our kids to the peace that comes from their own identities in Christ. Sonship is a place of release and empowerment for our kids. Like us, they are chosen, adopted, blessed with every spiritual blessing, citizens of heaven, sons of God, forgiven, justified, redeemed, hidden in Christ, righteous, accepted, worthy, holy, beloved, remade, and a delight to God.

PRAYER

Heavenly Father, forgive me for how I've invested my identity into my role as Mom or Dad. Thank you for the gift of letting me reflect your love to my children. Thank you for the humbling call to shepherd their hearts. Forgive me for receiving my worth from that role. Forgive me for my codependence. Forgive me for my idolatry. Forgive my fear and worry. Forgive my dismissiveness of you in their lives. Thank you that you have adopted me as your son. Thank you that even when we were enemies, you welcomed me into your home. Thank you for giving me your name and lavishing me with your mercy. Teach me to trust you as my Father and to entrust my children to you as their perfect Father. Teach me what intimacy with you looks like. Transform my heart to reflect your character as a parent. May I wake up every morning knowing the security of your adopting love in my life, and may that reality set me free to parent in love, truth, and grace. Amen.

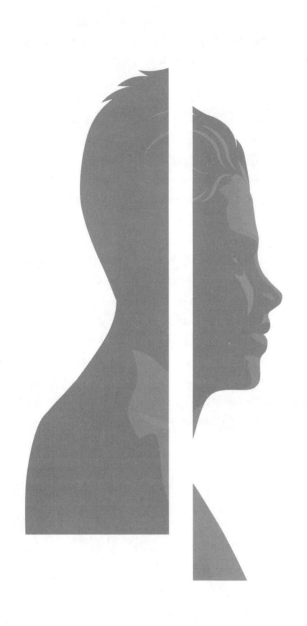

Ideologies
Finding Humility as Jesus's Friend

⌒

Like a surgeon, friends cut you in order to heal you.
—Tim and Kathy Keller

God doesn't just love you—he likes you.
—Brennan Manning

*No longer do I call you servants; for the servant does
not know what his master is doing;
but I have called you friends.*
—Jesus

JOHN

ANGEL SAT IN FRONT OF a muscle-bound client. He came in angry. He came in fearful. The recent election made him afraid his right to bear arms would be taken from him. "How dare anyone tell me I cannot carry a weapon. How dare anyone take my rights away from me."

☞

I listened as a congregant's voice trembled in rage on the other side of the phone line. "You're killing people!" she spat. "Their blood will be on your hands." She couldn't believe we would open our doors in any fashion, no matter what precautions we took, in the middle of the COVID-19 pandemic. She feared for children's health. "I will not attend a church where my pastors endanger babies' lives."

☞

In 2016, data scientists Eitan Hersh and Yair Ghitza analyzed data among registered voters to determine how often Democrats and Republicans married. They learned that 30 percent of couples were politically mixed, meaning they did not share the same party identification. However, most of those mixed marriages were between Independents and a spouse registered as Republican or Democrat. Only 9 percent of marriages were between Democrats and Republicans. That number has worsened. In 2020, the American Family Survey saw that only 21 percent of marriages were politically mixed, and fewer than 4 percent were between Democrats and Republicans.[1] The indications are that we tend to only have deep friendships with those who share our political ideology.

In 1958, Gallup Research asked respondents, "'If you had a daughter of marriageable age, would you prefer she marry a Democrat or Republican, all other things being equal?' The results: 18% of Americans said they would prefer their daughter to marry a Democrat, 10% preferred a Republican, and the majority didn't care." When Gallup asked the same question in 2016, the number of those who cared nearly doubled: "28% of respondents said they preferred their child to marry a Democrat and 27% a Republican."[2]

In 2017, after Trump won the presidential election, 10 percent of

Americans ended a romantic relationship because of different political views.[3]

Politics are divisive no matter what country you live in. England has been split over Brexit (leaving the European Union). France has been divided over immigration policies. And South Korea has massive political division between its younger and older residents and between those in urban and rural environments.[4]

Let's make this personal. What would your reaction be if you learned a close friend of yours voted for a different presidential candidate than you in each of the past three elections? How would you feel if you walked into a new friend's home and MSNBC was on the TV in their living room? How about Fox News? How would it impact your friendship?

We long to be around those who validate our opinions and share our worldview. It's not surprising, then, that our political allegiances have a significant impact on our friendships. We struggle to share deep relationships with those who have different political commitments.

So strong is our allegiance to our ideology, Facebook and Twitter have realized, that to even expose us to those who disagree with us is bad business. Facebook's algorithm feeds you more posts from friends you engage with and fewer posts from friends you don't respond to.

You see the post from a friend about how excited they are after their candidate won (and you voted for the other candidate). Your stomach tightens. Do you respond? Unlikely. You scroll past it. Will you see the next post they make? It's less likely now that you didn't respond to their celebratory post. And so Facebook nudges you one inch further away from each other. A few months later, you're not quite as close with this friend, and you might not even know why.

The echo chambers we live in form silently around us. They segregate us and form us into communities and friendships based on our political ideologies.

"You are Republican," your Facebook algorithm whispers in your ear. "You are a Democrat," your social circle chants. "You don't just believe in those political ideas; they are who you are," the world murmurs. Taking a side and defending it has become the norm in our society. Being with others like us feels safe, comfortable, protected from critique. But when we're in a place where we separate from others, where we only hear, "Yes, you're right," we stagnate and fail to grow. Our political substitute identities leave us self-righteous, angry, and unable to cope with life's reality: not everyone is like us, sees things the way we do, or wants the same things we do. If our happiness depends on being isolated from differing opinions, it is a false happiness.

What a Friend We Have in Jesus

Christ invites us into a new identity—that of a friend. This is not an identity rooted in our political association but an identity that is rooted in our kingdom association.

In the kingdom of heaven, there will be no independents, conservatives, or liberals. There will be no squabbles over the best way to rule; there will be no one who is disenfranchised and no systemic sin. We will live in a world where we each live in the fruit of love, joy, peace, patience, kindness, goodness, faithfulness, gentleness, and self-control. We will willingly lay down our rights. In this kingdom, our rights aren't necessary. There is one King. His name is Jesus, and in his kingdom we are friends of God. And Jesus invites us to be friends with one another.

Pause for a moment and think about what it might look like to live today as if a taste of heaven came down to earth in your own heart and mind. Imagine the peace of knowing you don't have to be right. That Jesus has right and wrong settled. Think how your friendships might change if you lived in the overflow of your friendship with Christ and not friendships established through political allegiance.

Imagine the peace of knowing you don't have to be right. That Jesus has right and wrong settled.

Your identity in Christ is that you are a friend—a friend of Jesus. You are special. You are set apart. And he delights in you . . . no matter what happens.

Is it hard to think of yourself as Jesus's friend? Perhaps it feels like you are being presumptuous or cavalier. Put yourself in the sandals of the disciples. You've been with Jesus for three years. You've walked alongside him on the dusty roads of Galilee. You've seen him cast out demons, perform miracles, preach with the authority of heaven, and take on those who create man-made systems of effort to create identity instead of having identity given, by grace, by God himself. You've even seen him raise a man from the dead.

But the ruling party is not at all happy. They want Jesus dead.

Instead of hiding, Jesus goes to Jerusalem. All the disciples are sure this means it's time to overthrow the Romans and reestablish the Davidic throne. But things get weird. The people fete him as their king, and yet he chooses to ride in on a humble donkey colt. There is no amassing of weapons, no late-night planning of what the overthrow will look like.

Jesus shares a Passover meal that begins with him on his knees with a towel and a basin of water. You're confused. Why is Rebbe washing our feet? Where is the servant who should be doing the lowest task? Your group settles down as Jesus leads you through an emotional Passover meal.

As the meal winds to a close, Jesus says, "Truly, truly, I say to you, one of you will betray me." How can that be? How can someone from this inner circle betray Jesus? "Lord, who is it?" Peter asks what everyone is wondering. "It is he to whom I will give this morsel of bread." Jesus turns to Judas, hands him the bread and urges him,

"What you are going to do, do quickly." And Judas leaves (see John 13:21–30).

Jesus watches Judas walk out the door. Jesus turns back to you and says, "A new commandment I give to you, that you love one another: just as I have loved you, you also are to love one another. By this all people will know that you are my disciples, if you have love for one another" (vv. 34–35).

In the very moment his friend is betraying him, Jesus doubles down on his call throughout his ministry: "Love one another."

Jesus leads you out toward the garden of Gethsemane. He continues his theme of loving one another, this time inviting you into friendship:

> This is my commandment, that you love one another as I have loved you. Greater love has no one than this, that someone lay down his life for his friends. You are my friends if you do what I command you. No longer do I call you servants, for the servant does not know what his master is doing; but I have called you friends, for all that I have heard from my Father I have made known to you. You did not choose me, but I chose you and appointed you that you should go and bear fruit and that your fruit should abide, so that whatever you ask the Father in my name, he may give it to you. These things I command you, so that you will love one another. (John 15:12–17)

Friends! No Matter What

Did you see it? Jesus has just been betrayed by one of his closest friends. His other friends are about to fall asleep on him in his hour of need, Peter will deny him, and all but John will leave him during his trial and crucifixion. And it is at *this* moment Jesus tells this group of cowardly, unfaithful men that they are his friends!

Jesus tells this group of cowardly, unfaithful men that they are his friends!

I love Westerns (not so much for Angel). One of my favorites is the 1993 film *Tombstone*. At its heart, *Tombstone* is a story of friendship. At one point in the movie, the physically and spiritually sick Doc Holliday unexpectedly shows up to support and protect Wyatt Earp from a band of outlaws. He is as pale as a ghost, seemingly on the verge of collapsing at any moment. One outlaw, surprised that this selfish man would act so selflessly, asks why he came. "Wyatt Earp's my friend," Holliday responds. The inquirer scoffs, "I got plenty of friends." Doc Holliday looks at him and, with deep sincerity, replies, "I don't." We all long for this kind of a friend.

Unfortunately even the best of friends on this earth let us down. But we have a friend who surpasses every earthly friend. One who will love us even when we royally mess up.

Do you know that you are God's friend? Here are three blessings of being God's friend: God likes you. God confronts you. And God wants you to be with him. Let's explore these blessings.

1. God Likes You

He doesn't just love you—he enjoys you.

Remember choosing teams on the playground in elementary school? The last kid standing was always chosen with a sigh and a dismissive gesture by the captain. "I guess I'll take John." For many of us, sometimes that last kid was us. It was a punch in the gut every time. Shame spoke, "I'm not worth it."

There are a few grocery stores we frequent. The store that is on our way home often runs short on produce. If we swing by on the way home to pick up an avocado for guacamole, we might have to choose between a few deep-brown, spongy ones or a handful of light green ones that are as hard as baseballs. Back home, we enter the kitchen and apologetically lay down the avocado. "Sorry. It was the best one left."

Many of us think God chooses us like that. He was hoping for someone more intelligent, someone who would read their Bible more, someone with amazing evangelistic gifts, someone who does everything right the first time, but instead he got us.

But God didn't hold his nose when he chose you. He wants to be with you (see God's tender words in Hos. 11:8–11). You're God's perfect avocado. (That ought to be on a T-shirt, don't you think?)

Brant Hansen speaks to our fear. "You suspect you're unlovable? He loves you. You wonder, deep down if anyone could really, truly know you and still want you? He knows you better than you know you. And He wants you."[5]

God doesn't just put up with you. He truly likes you.

God doesn't love us because he's unaware of our junk. He knows the mess of our hearts far better than we do, and he still loves us. We long to be known, and we long to be loved. Some of our deepest fears reside behind those longings. Will I be known? Will I be loved? Perhaps you have feared being known but not loved. Or maybe you have known the hollowness of being loved but not known. In those spaces, we are left empty. God has made us to be fully known and fully loved. God knows us perfectly. And loves us still.[6]

That's hard to believe, isn't it? The Being in the universe who knows you more intimately than any other being also loves you infinitely more than any other being. There is no need, then, to shield God from our true selves with wooden prayers or minimize or excuse our sin to him. We can come just as we are. We can express our hopes and dreams, our disappointments and frustrations, and the depths of our sin with complete transparency. He might not agree with you, but he isn't going to hold that against you.

Angel reflects on when she was trapped in adultery, held hostage by her sin:

> I had tried so many times to get out of this evil and vicious trap I created for myself. I was truly stuck. I wasn't walking with God; I had rejected God. There came a moment where, through the Spirit, God pierced my heart and brought repentance. I sat in the bathtub, weeping, and cried out, "God all I have to offer you is my shallow, wretched self. I've got nothing left. I need help." That was a defining moment for me. I was willing to step through the door of transparency with the Lord, acknowledging my need for him and the depth of my despair because of my sin. I was done trying to fix myself. I needed my sovereign friend to rescue me. I needed him to ignore how different I was than him. I needed him to care for me regardless. And he did.

We need God more than we'll ever know. Our most profound longing is for Jesus himself. We just live much of our lives not knowing it. We plaster over our deep longing for Jesus's pure friendship with the thin spackle of political allies. We think that our longing for friendship will be satisfied if we find enough people who agree with us on enough issues. We try to fill that longing with a growing list of friends on social media. We're never satisfied, but we are so afraid of being fully seen by the true Friend that we exchange genuine friendship for a shell of the real thing.

In that moment in the bathtub, Angel's Best Friend listened, smiled, and delighted in her. How can God delight in us? We know just how selfish, shallow, and self-righteous we can be. But God not only sees you, knows you, and loves you . . .

He likes you.

2. God Confronts You

Part of being a good friend is constructive confrontation. Think of which friends you are willing to confront. They must be pretty good friends for you to be willing to step outside your comfort zone in order to speak hard truths lovingly to them. This confrontation comes from a deep caring. From a heart that wants the best for someone. From a desire to see your friend thrive and grow and become an even more amazing person than he or she already is.

A friendship void of conflict is not a true friendship. And a workplace without conflict is hardly perfect. Its employees are swimming in the toxic waters of avoidance.

Have you ever found your zipper down in the middle of the day or discovered a piece of spinach wedged between your incisor and canine teeth? "How long was my zipper down?" you wonder. "How many people noticed that spinach?" "Do my coworkers not like me enough to point out those things?" Those are legitimate questions. It takes a measure of trust to confront.

As author Ken Sande reminds us in his important book *The Peacemaker,* conflict is an opportunity. He means it is an opportunity for truth and growth.[7] Tim and Kathy Keller say, "Like a surgeon, friends cut you in order to heal you. Friends become wiser together through a healthy clash of viewpoints."[8] The deepest friendships are built not through ideological twins but through those who care enough to lovingly disagree and grow together.

Author and widow Andrée Seu Peterson reflects on what she misses about marriage. Surprisingly, one of the things she misses most is healthy disagreement. She says,

> Depth perception is the single biggest thing I miss in marriage. I can live well enough without the other perks—Saturday movie date, someone to lift the sofa with me. But

what causes me to lumber about and walk into walls these days is the forfeiture of a perspective other than my own.

If personalities are colors, I see indigo and my husband always saw sunny yellow—which is the reason I married him in the first place. Together we could be a good start toward a rainbow. Thesis, antithesis, synthesis. Iron sharpening iron.[9]

God sees our selfishness, and he confronts us in love. He refuses to allow us to get away with sin just because he's nice. He's not a fake, superficial nice—he's *loving*, and he loves us enough to call us to be better. He is a true friend.

In our flesh, we push away those who disagree with us. It is so much easier to be in relationship with someone who nods their head when we rant about the latest political scandal. It's so much easier to form friendships on agreements around ideas and not through alliances of the heart.

God sees our selfishness, and he confronts us in love. He is a true friend.

The Lord deeply desires to confront us in any ideology that would move us away from his kingdom agenda and our choice to "unfriend" the image bearer of Christ in front of us because of our differences. He loves us enough to confront us. A spirit of arrogance and boasting is an abomination to him. We cannot be a friend of God and a hater of another. John the elder speaks to us bluntly: "If anyone says, 'I love God,' and hates his brother, he is a liar; for he who does not love his brother whom he has seen cannot love God whom he has not seen" (1 John 4:20).

God loves us enough to confront us.

3. God Wants You to Be with Him

Right before Jesus calls his disciples friends, he offers this beautiful promise: "In my Father's house are many rooms. If it were not so, would I have told you that I go to prepare a place for you?" (John 14:2).

The end of our story is that we get to spend eternity with God. God doesn't save you to eternal life so you can live it on your own, in whatever manner you see fit. Do you like the idea of being with God forever? That might be a good indicator of how good a friend God is to you. How do you think God feels about your living with him forever? If you think he rolls his eyes at the thought, then you probably don't understand how he feels about you.

The story of Scripture is the story of God going to great lengths to dwell with his people.

Consider it. Our triune God dwelled in perfect love, harmony, and community as the great three-in-one God. Yet his love so overflowed that he desired to create human beings to dwell with (Rev. 21:3; John 17:20–26).

When he created human beings, he did not stay far off and watch them like a child would watch an ant farm. Instead, he dwelled with them. He walked with Adam and Eve daily. Can you imagine those conversations? What did they talk about? Maybe they considered Adam and Eve's plans for the garden. Perhaps they discussed the names they had given the animals. Or maybe they sat side by side and watched sunrises and sunsets together, marveling with joy as the colors exploded across the horizon. Do you believe God wants to have those conversations with you?

God doesn't shut off ideological conversations with us. He invites us to take all our concerns to him. As we wrestle with him, he invites us to place our trust in him and to refocus on his kingdom. He invites us to assume a posture of humility, living bowed before him on our knees rather than raising our fists to others and him in defiance.

As a friend of God, I am free to trust in his sovereignty and goodness and in his promises to be faithful in every political storm.

God's Friends

We get glimpses of this walking-with relationship throughout Scripture. In Genesis we meet a man named Enoch. He walked obediently with God for 365 years. We remember our childhood pastor, Roger Barrier, speaking fondly of this fascinating one-line snapshot of Enoch's life in Scripture: "Enoch walked with God, and he was not, for God took him" (Gen. 5:24). Enoch's relationship with God must have been one of intimate devotion as he went from his life on earth to his life in eternity. He never died. God just took him. Who wouldn't want to be that kind of friend to God?

The chronicler picks up on this same theme of friendship between God and Abraham: "Did you not, our God, drive out the inhabitants of this land before your people Israel, and give it forever to the descendants of Abraham your friend?" (2 Chron. 20:7). "Even if you don't regard us, please remember your friend," the writer seems to be imploring. James echoes: "The Scripture was fulfilled that says, 'Abraham believed God, and it was counted to him as righteousness' —and he was called a friend of God" (James 2:23). Abraham's belief in God was no mere intellectual agreement, and his righteousness was no mere moral standing: he was a *friend* of God.

God and Moses also spoke as friends. "The LORD used to speak to Moses face to face, as a man speaks to his friend" (Exod. 33:11). Do you know this is what God wants with you? He wants to sit down and chat over coffee. He wants to be the one you call when you lose your job, mess up again, or just need to go laugh and dance because it can't get any worse.

We invite you to experience friendships not merely because of shared allegiances but because they mirror how God wants to relate to you. Your Creator and Savior likes you. Do you long to know him as a friend? As he calls you friend, he invites you to walk alongside others as friends.

The Good Portion

Outside of his apostles, three of Jesus's closest friends were the sibling group of Martha, Mary, and Lazarus. At one point, Martha is rushing around trying to serve her friend Jesus. And she is fed up. Her sister has ditched her hospitality obligations (a big deal in the Middle East) just to sit and talk to Jesus.

Mary sits at Jesus's feet. Only men who were the rabbi's disciples were supposed to sit there.[10] It was the place of intimate learning. But Mary doesn't care about social convention. She doesn't care what others think. She isn't concerned about all the housework that needs to be done. She wants to be with and learn from her Lord and teacher, Jesus.

Exasperated, Martha comes to Jesus: "Lord, do you not care that my sister has left me to serve alone? Tell her then to help me" (Luke 10:40). But Jesus has a very different perspective. Hear not just the rebuke but also the love and invitation in his response: "Martha, Martha, you are anxious and troubled about many things, but one thing is necessary. Mary has chosen the good portion, which will not be taken away from her" (vv. 41–42).

That's a funny little phrase: "good portion." Jesus is saying that when it comes to dinner, Mary has chosen the best dish: Jesus himself. Forget the music, forget the hors d'oeuvres, forget the roast, forget the salad, forget the bread, forget even dessert. Jesus is better than all of it.

This is where our faith and our Christian life begin and end: at Jesus's feet. We are called to come to his feet and listen. Put away your phone, turn off the music, grab your Bible, sit on your couch, and ask the Lord to meet you in his living Word and prayer. Ask him to bring truth, conviction, and transformation. Our posture of humility grows when we recognize our need for Jesus and make a choice to put aside distractions and regularly sit at his feet. We promise you, that's way better than scrolling on Facebook. Social media naturally leads us to self-condemnation and being judgmental. Political conversations with those aligned with us often have the unstated premise "How stupid can *they* be?" But friendship with Jesus draws us deeper into peace, unity, and humility. In the presence of Jesus, we are all too aware that we don't have the answers, but we are confident we know who does.

This is where our faith and our Christian life begin and end: at Jesus's feet.

Come to Jesus's feet and listen to what he says to you. You are not your worldview, your ideology, nor your political allegiance; you are a friend of God. Listen to what he says about his kingdom. Set your heart of friendship on that kingdom. Listen through reading the Bible. Listen through prayer. Listen through the preaching of God's Word. Listen through Christian brothers and sisters.

Come with a heart full of adoration for who he is: our wonderful Savior, our Creator, our Lord, our Healer, our Sustainer. But also come with all your hurts and pains. Tell him how angry you are with what is going on politically. Cry out over injustice. Beg for him to respond. Tell him about how frustrating it is that you can't get a good night's sleep. Share your weariness over trying to break your addiction; share with Jesus your sorrow over your children and grandchildren's poor choices, your hurt over past relationships. Be real. Come to Jesus. Come with ears ready to listen, come with all of who you are to him. He will listen. As you come to him, he will shape your hope in him.

The famous eighteenth-century pastor and hymn writer John Wesley was surrounded by his closest friends when he died. He ushered his friends close to him as he breathed his last. His final words were these: "Best of all, God is with us."

Best of all, God is with you. He leans in as your friend and invites you to lean into him. He delights in you and longs for you to find delight in him.

No matter where you are right now, he invites you, as a friend, to be a friend.

PRAYER

Best Friend, forgive me for allowing my political allegiance to define who I am. Forgive me that my ideology has shaped my friendship group. Forgive me for cutting out those I disagree with. Forgive me for not taking my frustrations to you. Forgive me for not praying more that your kingdom would come.

Best Friend, how often have I treated you more like an auditor than a friend? How often have I treated you like a police officer? How often have I missed the gifts of friendship you invite me into? Forgive me. Forgive me for choosing friends based on their ideology. Forgive me for not befriending those who think differently than me. Give me a longing to sit at your feet. Retrain me to come to you and pour out the highs and lows of my day as I would to my friend. Teach me to listen as a good friend does. As I learn to delight in our friendship, help me, Best Friend, to be a friend to those you put in my path. Amen.

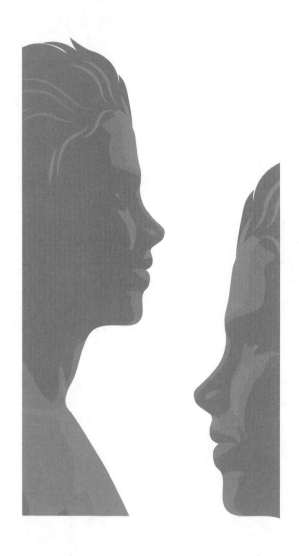

Career
Finding Purpose as a Gifted Member of God's Family

⌒

I'm a fighter pilot. . . . It's not what I am; it's who I am.
—Pete "Maverick" Mitchell, as played by
Tom Cruise in *Top Gun: Maverick*

'Tis very hard to behold our own gifts without pride, and the gifts of others without envy.
—Vavasor Powell

We are all talented people. Anything whereby we may glorify God is a talent.
—J. C. Ryle

ANGEL

JACOB SITS ACROSS FROM US, as far away from his wife as he can possibly be on the love seat. She demands that he apologize for the way he has prioritized his job over her and commit to change. His jaw sets. "If I am not a contractor, I don't know what I am. My employees treat me with respect, unlike you. I go to work, I build something, and I come home and get torn down. If you take my company away from me, I've got nothing. Why should I stay married to a woman who can't appreciate who I am?"

Randall is slumped in front of me, his six-foot, 250-pound frame somehow filling up only a tiny fraction of the love seat. He shares that he received a medical discharge from the military. "What am I going to do? I'm thirty-five years old, and I am completely lost. I'm overweight, I don't have a degree, and I'm jobless. I'm no good to anyone. I entered the military when I was eighteen. Who am I?"

"What do you want to be when you grow up?"

As we discussed in the introduction, this is a question every child is asked. The question isn't "What do you want to *do* when you grow up?" It's "What do you want to *be*?" The "be" reveals our cultural assumption: our identity is found in our vocation. We think our job is what defines who we are; we believe it gives us meaning and purpose.

Every one of us spends at least twelve years of education preparing for a job. Many of us spend an additional four, six, even ten years furthering our education for the job we feel called to. The average American spends 15 to 29 percent of his or her life in school.[1]

By the time we retire, we will have poured an average of ninety thousand hours into our work—a full third of our lives.[2] The only thing we spend more hours doing is sleeping.

When we meet someone, how do we start the conversation? One of the first questions we ask is, "What do you do?" And what they do probably changes what we think of them. A teacher might rise in our esteem while a car salesman might fall. Our estimation of a doctor's intelligence is likely higher than a handyman's. We're likely to assume a social worker is more honest than a politician.

We think our job is what defines who we are; we believe it gives us meaning and purpose.

Our esteem of ourselves is often impacted by our vocation. How many of us have poured ourselves out to nail that project, achieve a promotion, or have our dream employer extend us an offer, only to feel empty on the other side? What difference did we really make? Why do we feel like imposters?

One of John's first jobs was working maintenance at a cement plant. He reflects on his time there:

> It was hard work. I would come home physically exhausted, caked in cement dust. My skin was constantly irritated, my body ached. Our ragtag maintenance crew was at the bottom of the cement plant's hierarchy, and we were largely ignored by the skilled workers. A decade later, on the day of my ordination, I stood before the congregation as my mentors laid hands on me in prayer. I was the same person, but did I feel the same measure of worth when I swept out cement silos as I did when I received the title "Reverend"? I wish I could say I did, but my heart had far too much of its worth invested in my vocation for that to be the case. In my flesh, I felt more important on my ordination day than I did as a cement factory groundskeeper.

It is problematic to connect the umbilical cord of worth to the womb of our vocation. To do so is to give our employer power over our self-worth. What happens when we don't get the promotion we thought we deserved? What do we speak over ourselves when we don't perform?

I want to highlight vocation with a bit of a twist. This book reflects roles that we turn into identities. This chapter, however, attempts to explain that we do have a vocational identity. We just shrink it down from what God intends it to be. We will navigate how vocation is part of your true identity, and then dig into how we manipulate God's intended identity. Let's begin.

Dominion

When God decided to create human beings, he set them apart by making them in his image. There are many ways we reflect the image of God, but the very first is the dominion we have. Look at how closely the image of God and our vocation are linked in Genesis 1:26, "God said, 'Let us make man in our image, after our likeness. And let them have dominion over the fish of the sea and over the birds of the heavens and over the livestock and over all the earth and over every creeping thing that creeps on the earth.'" God creates human beings as the crown jewel of his creation, imaging his likeness to the world. And what is the first way they reflect God? Through their dominion over God's creation.

Consider God's first words to Adam and Eve: "Be fruitful and multiply and fill the earth and subdue it, and have dominion over [it]" (v. 28). We were made for dominion.

What is dominion? In Genesis 1 and 2, four Hebrew words are used to describe Adam and Eve's relationship with the garden. They are to rule over it (*radah*), subdue it (*kabash*), till it (*abad*), and keep it (*shamar*). Taken together, we see that Adam and Eve are given kingly and queenly reign over the garden, purposed to lead by stewarding and caring for the gift God has given them. They are to be benevolent and generous leaders.

We were made to rule, to steward, to create, to organize, and to care. We were made to work.

God gives each of us this same invitation. We are to image him as we rule over our world with charity and understanding. Wherever God calls us, we are to improve that ground. The neighborhoods we live in ought to be better because of our dominion. The workplaces we dwell in ought to be more loving and organized because of our presence. The schools we learn at ought to be more caring and more honest.

> ## We were made to work. Wherever God calls us, we are to improve that ground.

But doesn't God curse Adam with work when he sins by eating of the Tree of Knowledge of Good and Evil? Not quite. The curse for Adam's sin is not that he will work; he is already working. God's curse on Adam is that, for the first time, his work will be difficult (Gen. 3:17–19). He's going to battle thorns and thistles, and his work is going to make him sweat. After a long day of labor, Adam's hands will blister and his shoulders will ache. He will be frustrated as mislaid bricks cause the walls to cave in. But in heaven, we will experience work restored (and even better than the work Adam experienced). It will be fulfilling, exciting, and purposeful.

We've all had a glimpse of this promise in our lives. Even in some of our early jobs, we experience the satisfaction of purposeful work. John remembers creating his own twist of a dish when he worked as a chef in a fast-food Japanese restaurant in high school. I worked as the cashier and was delighted to gobble down John's new creations.

I remember the satisfaction of waitressing at Cracker Barrel, watching exhausted laborers at the end of their workday relax in their chairs, fill their bellies with apple butter biscuits and chicken fried steak, and leave satisfied. John recalls his feeling of accomplishment when, as a detention officer, he deep cleaned, restocked, and reorganized the officer's tower. And I can still see the smile on the face of a single mom preparing for a job interview when, while working at The Gap, I created the perfect outfit for her. And of course, John and I have both known many powerful moments of joy as a pastor and a counselor.

Charles Spurgeon once asked his congregation, "Do you know, dear friends, the deliciousness of work?"[3] Do you? You will!

We are Christ's workmanship, vessels prepared "for honorable use, set apart as holy, useful to the master of the house, ready for every good work" (2 Tim. 2:21). Our work on this side of eternity will not go to waste, and we have the gift of working for the rest of eternity.

Our Vocation Is Too Small

But the story of our calling doesn't end here. We see in the New Testament that God has a particular vocation for us, not just in terms of our job but also in relation to the church. Recognizing the powerful and fresh new work of the Holy Spirit after Christ's ministry, the New Testament writers saw our vocation as believers in the context of Christ's body.

The problem, then, isn't that we understand we were made to image God through our work; the problem is that our understanding of our vocation is too limited. We were made not just for vocation in the world but also for vocation in the community of believers.

The King Bears Gifts

What is the most amazing gift you could be given? God has offered us the best gifts we can imagine. In the book of Ephesians, Paul gives us a cosmic description of the conquering work of Jesus on the cross. He pictures Jesus as an ancient conquering king, returning victorious from war with treasure chests of loot. In Jesus's ultimate dominion over dark forces, he spreads the wealth of his victory to the church. What is that wealth Jesus distributes? It is the treasure of the Spirit. And who are the beneficiaries of these gifts? We are.

But there is a twist. Every gift given by our benevolent king isn't given for ourselves; it is given for others. Paul shares a unique perspective on how salvation and God's gifts are connected. He explains:

> Grace was given to each one of us according to the measure of Christ's gift. Therefore it says,
>> "When he ascended on high he led a host of captives,
>> and he gave gifts to men." . . .
> And he gave the apostles, the prophets, the evangelists, the shepherds and teachers, to equip the saints for the work of ministry, for building up the body of Christ, until we all attain to the unity of the faith and of the knowledge of the Son of God, to mature manhood, to the measure of the stature of the fullness of Christ. (Eph. 4:7–8, 11–13)

God conquers and then showers the gifts of his victory on you. And those gifts are primarily given for the sake of the family of God.

The Gift Giver

Our daughter is an amazing gift giver. She puts unbelievable energy into the gifts she gives. She has painted friends watercolor pictures that speak encouragement to them. She has spent hours making them handcrafted gifts, sometimes even as a joke to make them laugh. Even as we write this, she is next to us embroidering a bookmark to give to a friend. To top it off, Camille's presents come beautifully wrapped with handcrafted cards. We love unwrapping her gifts. Each one speaks of her character and her care for us. We love watching others unwrap her gifts as well. Her gift can be hidden amid a pile of gifts, and yet, when her present is opened, the frenzy stops. The recipient slows down, recognizing the meaningfulness of Camille's gift.

Such are our heavenly Father's gifts. They speak of his care and his character. Every gift we receive, whether it is the gift of service or teaching or mercy, speaks to the character of its Giver.

We often overlook the Giver when we talk about gifts in the church. As we pointed out in chapter 4, a proliferation of personality profiles is available today. We imagine you've probably done at least one of them—the Myers-Briggs, perhaps, or CliftonStrengths, or Enneagram, or DiSC. They're fun tests, and they're helpful. It's a good thing to better understand yourself. It's a good thing to be able to lean into how God has uniquely wired you and to grow in self-understanding. We believe God wants us to do so. In some ways, you could consider the lists of gifts in the Bible a sort of first-century CliftonStrengths.

> **Every gift we receive, whether it is the gift of service or teaching or mercy, speaks to the character of its Giver.**

Usually, the gifts God gives fit the natural personality and aptitude of an individual. There are certainly exceptions, but for most of us, our spiritual gifting is connected to the natural aptitudes God has given us.

Paul says God rescued us for good works that he designed for us to step into. After speaking of God's unmerited rescue of us, Paul says, "We are his workmanship, created in Christ Jesus for good works, which God prepared beforehand, that we should walk in them" (Eph. 2:10). When God formed and fashioned you, he did so with a plan in mind to accomplish good works through you. In Christ we all have a general calling to glorify God and enjoy him forever. We all also have unique gifts to receive from the Gift Giver and bring into the vocational land in which we dwell. My good works are different from your good works. You were created with a particular personality and unique abilities to accomplish good things God designed for you. Whether you're a waitress at Cracker Barrel, a maintenance crew member at a cement plant, a landscaper, an artist, or a lawyer . . . wherever you abide vocationally, you are purposed in that space for the glory of God. Don't let your opportunity go to waste.

Should we just stack spiritual gifts alongside all the other evaluations of personality and strengths? Yes and no. On the one hand, the better we can understand who God has made us to be, the better we will be able to step into the calling he has on our lives. On the other hand, spiritual gifts point us to significant truths that are often lost in personality tests. Whereas personality tests have us focus on how to improve ourselves, with a better understanding of our personality (not a poor goal), considering spiritual gifts calls us to look first to their Giver. The gifts tell us something about God.

God Is Generous

The gifts speak of God's care for us. They speak of his attributes. Just as when we receive gifts at Christmas, we appropriately give thanks to their giver, so too does God want us to press into our relationship with him in gratitude. Our gifts ought to remind us of his generosity. And when we trust in God's generosity, we can walk in peace in our vocational purpose. We don't have to strive and strain, thinking our livelihood depends on us. God has gifted us vocationally, and he is generous. He will provide.

God Is Perfect Community

When Paul writes to the dysfunctional church at Corinth, he turns to the question of their giftings in 1 Corinthians 12. This is a church where the giftings of the members of the body have been weaponized. The congregants are using their gifts for selfish reasons and to elevate those who have them.

Paul begins, "Now there are varieties of gifts, but the same Spirit; and there are varieties of service, but the same Lord; and there are varieties of activities, but it is the same God who empowers them all in everyone. To each is given the manifestation of the Spirit for the common good" (vv. 4–7).

Why are the gifts given? For the common good. The gifts we receive are not for ourselves but for someone else.

Because our triune God exists in perfect, eternal community, it is no surprise that the gifts he gives us are intended to strengthen others and expand his kingdom. God has blessed us to be a blessing. God has served us so we can serve others. God has loved us so we can love others. Because our gifts are intended for the blessing of others, God gently nudges us into community with the gifts he blesses us with. Like a parent purchasing a basketball hoop and setting it up in the cul-de-sac with the intention of gathering the neighborhood kids, God gives us gifts to draw us into relationship with our brothers and sisters in Christ. And those relationships point us back to our triune God in perfect community.

God has blessed us to be a blessing.

And yet how many of us sit on the sidelines of our God-given communities? We attend a couple times a month and give whatever we feel we are able, but who is benefiting from our presence? Who is benefiting from our ministry? We may send money to faraway places, but we neglect our neighbors and our local Christian community. We may pray for missionaries in Africa but neglect to take meals to the family whose mother was just diagnosed with cancer.

Or we may write brilliantly phrased opinions on Facebook but neglect lovingly calling our friend out for disrespecting his wife in public. We use our gifts, but at arm's length where there is little risk.

Our gifts are a ministry calling for the ultimate purpose of God's glory (1 Peter 4:10–11). We each strive to be our very best and then give out of that strength to others so that the world is drawn to an amazing God. But if we hide our gifts, we also hide God's glory.

If you aren't using your gifts for the benefit of God and his people, you are misappropriating the most important gift God gave you at salvation. A couple of our friends have nice company trucks. Their jobs necessitate quite a bit of travel and the ability to carry heavy equipment and navigate difficult terrain. If they quit their jobs but kept the trucks, their bosses would be rightfully indignant. The trucks are *for the job.*

But this is the spiritual reality of many Christians. Many who claim to follow Christ are not actively serving. Fellow Christians, we are no better than the guy with the company truck who quit the company. God gave us gifts for the purpose of his people. Are we using them for that purpose?

God Is Our Equipper

We don't serve in our own strength. Looking to the Equipper gives us permission not to strive but to trust that he has equipped us and purposed us for where we are placed in our families, churches, and vocations. The author of Hebrews prays a benediction over those he writes to, asking that Jesus "equip you with everything good that you may do his will" (Heb. 13:21). Drawing from the Old Testament tradition of pouring oil over the head of a newly appointed king to set him aside for his calling, the early church had a tradition of anointing those who were newly baptized for the purpose of their spiritual service in the household of God. Just as David was anointed for his service as king, the oil of anointing spills over our heads. God's Spirit in us is that oil (Luke 4:18; Acts 10:38). God equips us through the Spirit.

Giving Ourselves

In Romans 12, Paul reflects on what it looks like to enter into a relationship with Christ. In the first portion of the passage, Paul commends us to give ourselves first to God. You might be familiar with this portion, a call to present our bodies as living sacrifices. That's not where the passage ends, though. We are not to give ourselves to God alone; God will give us to his family.

Listen to Paul:

> I appeal to you therefore, brothers, by the mercies of God, to present your bodies as a living sacrifice, holy and acceptable to God, which is your spiritual worship. Do not be conformed to this world, but be transformed by the renewal of your mind, that by testing you may discern what is the will of God, what is good and acceptable and perfect. (vv. 1–2)

Isn't that interesting? The passage runs counter to the way we are conditioned to think about faith: It isn't a way to improve our lives. Faith certainly benefits us, but it also costs us everything, starting with ourselves.

Paul continues, sharing that part of our faith journey is growing in humility. One of the ways God develops humility in us is in the context of community. We are not made to go on this spiritual journey alone. The call to individual commitment is never left just between the believer and God. God calls us to himself, and then he gives us to the church.

> By the grace given to me I say to everyone among you not to
> think of himself more highly than he ought to think, but to
> think with sober judgment, each according to the measure
> of faith that God has assigned. (v. 3)

While our gifts have been given to us for the sake of others, the
inverse is also true: We are dependent on the gifts of others in our
lives. This is the outflow of grace from God through us to his bride.

> As in one body we have many members, and the members
> do not all have the same function, so we, though many,
> are one body in Christ, and individually members one of
> another. Having gifts that differ according to the grace
> given to us, let us use them: if prophecy, in proportion to
> our faith; if service, in our serving; the one who teaches, in
> his teaching; the one who exhorts, in his exhortation; the
> one who contributes, in generosity; the one who leads, with
> zeal; the one who does acts of mercy, with cheerfulness. (vv.
> 4–8)

God is rich in his mercy and in the blessings he gives his children, so it is not surprising that when God gives us to the church,
he blesses us by handing us over to his bride. We don't go to church
to minimize stress or to be happier, yet it isn't surprising that those
who attend church are happier and have lower levels of stress. Why
shouldn't they? If they are at church for the right reasons, they are
there because they have given themselves to their Creator and now
are functioning in the way they are called to function. They are
truly human. Their identity fits with reality. Of course, happiness
increases and stress decreases when we honor the purposes our
Creator designed us for.

A Spiritual Gym

We tend to have a high view of individual spirituality, and we see our communal experiences of spirituality as being there merely to enhance our personal spiritual health—kind of like a spiritual gym. When we go to the gym, others there can seem like obstacles to our physical health, using the weights and machines we want to use. We smile on days when we walk in and see we've got the whole row of elliptical machines or the thirty-minute workout zone to ourselves. The only benefit of other human beings in the gym is the general sense of camaraderie that we are in this together. Oh, and it's always nice to have a trainer within spitting distance if we don't know how to use a particular machine. We appreciate that the employees smile when they check us in, and put on nice music, and clean up the equipment. But in general, we know what we need to do. We just need to muster up the gumption and try harder.

Isn't this consumption mentality how most of us think of church? What purpose do the other people at your church have? It's nice to have someone greet us at the door. But let's make sure we don't get too personal, please. Some good atmospheric music to get us in the mood is a plus, though if it isn't our style, we can always show up late. It's good to have the trainer—er, the pastor—coach us and give us a few tips. And let's be sure the maintenance guy keeps things spic-and-span.

But that isn't what God intends. The church is meant to be more like a training group for a relay team. We work to strengthen ourselves, but the rest of the team depends on us too. We are each absolutely necessary to one another. Each contributes, and each spurs the others on. Our Creator made us in such a way that we are most fulfilled and most satisfied when, having given ourselves to him, we let him give us to the church.

Thy Paycheck Come

The danger in allowing our vocations rather than our giftings to be the source of our identity is that we disregard who God is and whom he has called us to be. We shrink his calling to how we earn a paycheck. When we dismiss God's purposes for our gifts, we functionally make our jobs our gods. We miss out on the peace and joy God has for us in our occupational calling. We miss out on the fulfillment of blessing others. We miss out on the blessing of experiencing God's sovereignty over our finances and jobs. If our only purpose is the paycheck, we dismiss the opportunity to serve the image bearers in front of us. We miss the opportunity to bring glory to God.

For how many of us is this our true prayer: "My job is my shepherd; I shall not want. It drives me until I can't go any more. It destroys my soul"? Or, "Our job, which art in Tucson, you are my everything. Thy paycheck come; thy will be done in my home as it is in my workplace. Give us today our daily bread." Vocational identity on our own terms is functional atheism. Vocation may be one of our true identities, but when we misunderstand our vocations, it is destructive to our souls.

John reflects on his own functional atheism:

> When I graduated from seminary, I plunged myself headlong into vocational ministry. Feeling the drive to establish myself and curry honor from my congregation, my hours at the church ballooned and my time with Angel and the kids shrank. "It's just a season," I promised, but the months passed, and my family felt the pain of my neglect. I was functionally married to another woman, and her demands were limitless. Even in the context of the church, I twisted my calling into an idol, craving the respect of the congregation. I understood my call, but I had wrongly prioritized

the communal bride over my one-flesh bride. I stewarded my gifts for the sake of self (earned respect) rather than trusting the Giver of the gifts within the boundaries he set for his glory and the good of his bride. To be clear, God did intend for my gifts to be used for the good of his church, but the church is *his* bride, not mine. It was an indication of a deceived and sick soul that my worth was tethered to how the church valued me.

You have been given gifts by the Giver. With those gifts comes a calling—a calling to God's people. That is the hidden vocation so many of us are neglecting. Your responsibility is to identify those gifts and then figure out whom you get to bless with them.[4]

When I first stepped into my calling as a counselor after my graduation, I would have told you, "I *am* a counselor, and I am responsible for those who step into my office. It is my job to relate to them and to take their challenges into my hands and help. If I don't, I will be a failure." Failing God's calling on my life was a burden I felt daily: the shame of my inability to fix counselees.

You have been given gifts by the Giver. With those gifts comes a calling.

What foolishness! The Enemy convinced me it was in my power to ensure I was a good counselor. I believed him. And because fixing others is not in our power, his lies led me into a season of overwhelming exhaustion, anxiety, and despair.

That season ultimately turned self-destructive. Taking on the responsibility for others is crushing. Despair is painful, and I fought hard to escape it. By God's grace, to walk through healing, he led me out of my role as a counselor. Once he restored me to himself, he graciously allowed me to return to counseling, although my approach is now entirely different. I know I am gifted by the King with a gift for his people. He calls me to this vocation not for myself but for God and for his bride. I do not counsel in my wisdom. I do not offer my truth. There isn't a single situation or person I can fix. I am simply an agent to give wisdom that comes from God alone, for the edification of the person sitting in front of me. I willingly say yes to being a living sacrifice for Jesus as he, and he alone, moves through me in power to transform and sanctify the gifted saint I sit across from. I am now deployed to help those whom God brings to me. Submitting to God and his purpose for me with my gifts is the vocational path of peace.

God has gifted you vocationally. Your job is to trust him to use you for his glory and your good in the home, marketplace, and church. Trust him and his purposes. God has uniquely designed you to steward his kingdom's purposes and represent Jesus to the world around you in his strength, not your own. How might God be calling you to have your vocational calling bless your spouse? Your children? Your family? Your neighbors? Your church? Our vocational gifts have a rightful order in our lives and a purpose to bless others. Let's not twist them into false identities that end up drowning ourselves and the people around us.

PRAYER

Thank you for the gift of bearing your image in my particular dominion, Lord of all. Thank you that you have given me a vocational calling. Forgive me for functionally believing that I am what I do for a living. Gift Giver, thank you for your gifts! Forgive me for how I have received your gifts. I've received them as a spoiled child, entitled and uncaring. I have not used my gifts for the purpose you intended: the blessing of others. Give me your infectious gift-giving heart. Give me eyes to see those who could benefit from the gifts you have given me. Give me your joy when I offer those gifts to others. Give me a renewed sense of calling to your bride that is rightly prioritized. I know I have been given much, and much is required of me. I surrender myself to be a living sacrifice for you in the vocational land you have made me to dwell in as it pleases you. Amen.

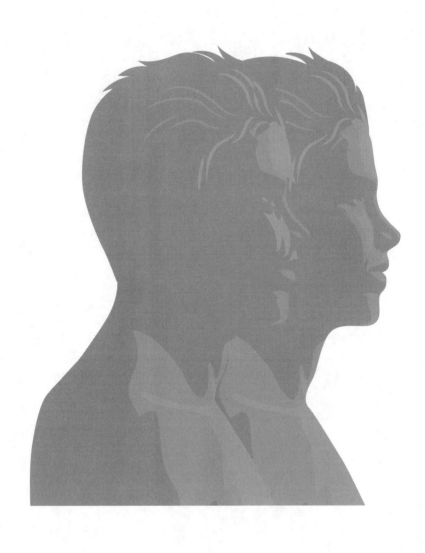

Patriotism
Finding Boldness as an Ambassador of Christ

⌐

*Let every nation know . . . that we shall pay any price,
bear any burden, meet any hardship, support any friend,
oppose any foe in order to assure the survival and the
success of liberty.*
—John F. Kennedy

*For here we have no lasting city, but we seek the city
that is to come.*
—the author of Hebrews

*Our citizenship is in heaven, and from it we await
a Savior, the Lord Jesus Christ.*
—Paul

TRADING FACES

JOHN

FRANK WORE A BEAT-UP "VIETNAM Vet" hat and a "Proud to be an American" shirt. "I'm just so angry," he told me after a service. "I gave up everything for our country. It's the greatest nation in the world. And this generation is so spoiled. They're throwing it all away. I feel like I'm losing everything I gave my life for."

On another day I approached Robert, a godly man in our congregation. "Would you consider joining our short-term missions team? I think you would be such an encouragement to the pastors there." He tilted his head, "But it's so dangerous there. I would never leave America to go to a place like that. There's too much risk."

~

Every American born before 1995 probably remembers where they were on September 11, 2001. Angel and I were in our small apartment outside Phoenix, Arizona. We watched the images of a plane striking the World Trade Center on our small television.

In the days that followed, the nation transformed. Eyes were glued on televised presidential speeches, flags hung from porches and cars, and "God Bless America" was inserted into the seventh inning of baseball games. What we once took for granted, we didn't take for granted any longer. We were proud to be Americans.

A decade later, on May 2, 2011, Angel and I sat in Citizens Bank Park watching the Phillies square off against the Nationals. A strange murmur started spreading through the stadium. We looked at each other trying to figure out what was going on. It was unlike the regular murmur of a sports game. Chants of "USA! USA!" started breaking out, softly at first. We turned to look behind us, and a Phillies fan, seeing our confusion, said, "We got him. Osama bin Laden is dead." The chants grew louder. A greater unity than sports was present: the love of country.

~~~

Our friends Keith and Madhu grew up in southern India, where Keith was a surgeon and Madhu was a dermatologist. They came with their eighteen-year-old son Ajit to the United States in 2001 to visit their daughter and son-in-law. Ajit was born with a life-threatening congenital abnormality, and while in the United States, his condition worsened. In order to care for Ajit, the couple made sacrifices in their careers and sought accommodations to stay in the country. Keith received a work visa, and Ajit was able to receive medical and educational support. By God's grace, Ajit lives today. We think of other friends who have come to America for greater opportunities or political stability. Not every story has a happy ending, but many do.

It is a good thing to love the country you call home. Good Christians are called to be good citizens.

It is a good thing to love the country you call home. Good Christians are called to be good citizens. Peter exhorted Christians living under an oppressive ruler to honor him (1 Peter 2:17). Similarly, Jeremiah urged Jews living in exile in Babylon to "seek the welfare of the city where I have sent you into exile, and pray to the LORD on its behalf, for in its welfare you will find your welfare" (Jer. 29:7).

Both Peter and Jeremiah are really saying that if you have a relationship with God, you ought to be a patriot: committed to the best for your city and your nation, even if they are working against you.

Patriotism can be beautiful, reflecting a reverence for God in one's commitment to one's nation. But we are not our nationality. Our identity is not found in our country of origin. It is found in our country of destiny: God's eternal kingdom.

A Life Verse

When God rescued Angel out of her season of adultery, Psalm 51 became her life passage. David's psalm of repentance begins:

> Have mercy on me, O God,
>   according to your steadfast love;
> according to your abundant mercy
>   blot out my transgressions.
> Wash me thoroughly from my iniquity,
>   and cleanse me from my sin! (vv. 1–2)

David's cry for mercy became Angel's daily cry for mercy.

Later in the passage, David makes it clear that his repentance doesn't just remain between himself and God. He says he will trumpet the invitation to repentance to all around him ("Then I will teach transgressors your ways, and sinners will return to you," v. 13). God's mercy results in David's proclamation of the Lord's character.

Like David, we have been rescued and redeemed by the blood of the Lamb in order to invite others to turn from sin and return to Jesus. When you and I experience God's transformation, he sends us out as ambassadors. Angel is not merely forgiven; she is an ambassador of Jesus, inviting others to godly repentance.

It was two weeks before college started. I chose Gordon College, a small school 2,500 miles away from my hometown in Tucson, Arizona, where I had only one acquaintance. I deplaned at Logan International in Boston, took public transportation to the bus stop, and headed with a cohort of incoming freshmen for two weeks of backpacking on the Appalachian Trail.

Every night by the campfire, one of us would share our life story along with our life verse. I didn't have a life verse, so I began to root through the Bible looking for an appropriate one as the days ticked down to my night to share.

Reading through Paul's letter to the Ephesians, I got to the part at the end where Paul asks the Ephesian church to pray for him. Out from Paul flows not just a request but a profound statement of his purpose. The words leaped off the page at me as if they were bolded and underlined. This was my purpose too. Paul says, "Keep alert with all perseverance, making supplication for all the saints, and also for me, that words may be given to me in opening my mouth boldly to proclaim the mystery of the gospel, for which I am an ambassador in chains, that I may declare it boldly, as I ought to speak" (Eph. 6:18–20).

This is my life mission: to boldly declare the gospel as an ambassador of Jesus Christ. David's call to be an ambassador isn't just a call he and Angel share. Paul's call is not merely a call he and I share. The call to be an ambassador is a call all believers share.

Before we dig into Ephesians 6 a little more, let's understand why we are all ambassadors.

Kingdom Citizenship

Near the end of his earthly ministry, Jesus prayed this truth over his disciples: "They are not of the world, just as I am not of the world" (John 17:16). One chapter later, Jesus stands before Pilate, accused of claiming to be the king of the Jews. Jesus answers, "My kingdom is not of this world. If my kingdom were of this world, my servants would have been fighting, that I might not be delivered over to the Jews. But my kingdom is not from the world" (18:36).

Our King's kingdom is not of this world. Our first citizenship is a heavenly citizenship. Have you ever been frustrated with someone you disagree with politically and felt the need to set that person straight? An acquaintance's social media video flashes across your phone with a snarky political hot take. Do you respond? Unlikely. But it's tempting. Jesus is so misunderstood that he is crucified. Yet his eyes are on a bigger kingdom and a bigger purpose. When we live as ambassadors, it isn't that we don't care about politics, but the heat and urgency lessen dramatically. The panicked cries that *this* is the most important election grow quiet.

Our first citizenship is a heavenly citizenship.

Peter profoundly understands this. He begins his first letter with this introduction: "Peter, an apostle of Jesus Christ, to those who are elect exiles of the Dispersion in Pontus, Galatia, Cappadocia, Asia, and Bithynia." Peter first identifies himself as an apostle—in Greek, *apostolos*, meaning, literally, a "sent-out-one." The word can also be translated as "messenger," "envoy," or "ambassador." Peter himself is an ambassador, sent from the kingdom of God to proclaim the good news of the transformative work of Jesus Christ to the nations of this world.

Peter next identifies those he is writing to. They live in what today is Turkey and are "elect exiles." Peter is drawing from the rich biblical imagery of the Israelites, who, upon the fall of Israel's Northern and Southern Kingdoms between the eighth and sixth centuries BC, were scattered around the ancient Near East as exiles. They lived as foreigners in alien lands. Their true allegiance was to a different kingdom.

Peter picks up the language of exiles for those he is pastoring, not because they are exiles of Israel but because they are exiles of the kingdom of God. As a matter of fact, we all are. Do you see the move Peter has made? He identifies himself as an apostle (literally, "sent one"), the highest and most authoritative role in the early Christian church. But then he calls them "elect exiles" (1 Peter 1:1). What is an "elect exile"? One purposefully sent out from their native land.

In other words, they also are apostles (sent ones). That's us. That's *you*. You are a citizen of heaven living on foreign soil. Not only that, but while you might think you are an outsider, an exile, a foreigner without rights, you are actually an ambassador.

Peter's words elevate every Christian. An ambassador, after all, was one of the most powerful people in ancient Rome. An ambassador was the emperor's voice and presence and had to be treated as such.

Love Your Temporary Home

Usually, ambassadors are chosen because of their relationship with the home country's emperor or king or president. That makes sense because the head of state sends the ambassador to represent him. An ambassador not only ensures that perfunctory duties are accomplished, but his or her presence conveys the leader's presence.

Ambassadors are also typically chosen because they have a connection with the place they serve. They need to know the language and customs, love the food, and embrace the culture. An ambassador who hates the place where she lives doesn't succeed. A few years ago, Spain's ambassador to Belgium was dismissed because he disliked Belgium and made no attempt to make connections with the Belgian government. "The worst of it is that he didn't represent the country at all," an embassy source said. "No one comes here. Matellanes [the ambassador] doesn't have meetings with anyone, he does nothing and prevents staff from taking even the smallest initiative."[1] Ouch. Instead, Matellanes spent his time making connections and inroads with the Vatican. He wasn't called to serve as ambassador to the Vatican. Matellanes was placed in Belgium to serve as a bridge between Spain and Belgium. Spending his efforts building bridges to the Vatican was a dereliction of duty and denied the purpose the Spanish government placed on his shoulders. You must serve as ambassador to the people and land God calls you to.

In Jeremiah, besides promising ultimate restoration to Israel,

God tells his people to inhabit the land they are dwelling in and make it better. We are not merely street preachers, proclaiming how vile our surroundings are. We are not simply messengers of destruction. We are salt and light. We are preserving agents representing our Most High King. We are to make things taste good. And because the Light is in us, we shine light to point the way to goodness and truth, and we take that light with us wherever we go.

> **Because the Light is in us, we shine light to point the way to goodness and truth.**

This pulls us right back to the preceding passage in Ephesians 6 where Paul reminds us that it isn't with people, with flesh and blood, that we struggle; our struggle is with the principalities of our enemy. So, when you come up against opposition as an ambassador of heaven, remember that your opponent is not those you are delivering the message to. Your opponent is Satan's empire.

We do not further our cause as ambassadors when we show a distaste for the place where we live. We lose credibility if we are ungrateful citizens of our cities, states, and countries. Be grateful for the unique beauty of the place God has called you to. We've had the opportunity to live in Arizona, Massachusetts, and New Jersey, and each has a special place in our hearts. Each is stunning in its own way. The land God has called you to is lovely. Don't be a grousing ambassador. Citizens of the kingdom are not made by complaints and boycotts. Remember, you represent the King, Jesus Christ. Every square inch of this earth was crafted by him, and he delights in it.

Becoming a Messenger

While the ambassador is powerful, he doesn't have unbridled power. His authority is a derivative authority. The ambassador must represent the leader, so the words the ambassador speaks have to be the leader's words, not his own. The ambassador can't make up the message he is going to give. If the ambassador is afraid the people would be upset by the message he's been sent to deliver, he can't water it down or smooth off its rough edges; he must deliver the message, the whole message, and nothing but the message.

Let's return to Paul's reflection on ambassadorship in his letter to the Ephesians. Paul has just written what will be his final words to the churches he planted in Turkey. The letter is written from prison in Rome, where Paul awaits his trial, sentencing, and martyrdom. Now an old man and an elder statesman of the gospel, Paul asks the Ephesian believers to pray for him. In doing so, Paul gives the business-card version of his life: who he is and what he's called to do. In doing so, he also tells us who we are and what we're called to do.

Let's remind ourselves what he says.

Boldness

Stand back and realize how amazing it is that Paul asks for prayer. Paul, of all people! *The* Paul. But he knows he needs prayer, and the content of his request is even more surprising. He asks for the things at the center of his ministry, his bread and butter: prayer for him "boldly to proclaim the mystery of the gospel" (Eph. 6:19). Paul, the first one who would be carved onto the Mount Rushmore of evangelists, is asking for prayer about evangelism.

We don't know how you feel about your ability to articulate the gospel, but we guarantee ours is significantly worse than Paul's. If Paul was asking for prayer that he be a bold evangelist, we ought to request prayer for that too.

So, what specifically should we pray for? First, for boldness to deliver the gospel with belief and courage. As ambassadors we are called to deliver the message as if it were ours. Have you ever had a supervisor who threw his boss under the bus whenever he had bad news to share? He owned the good news, but when it was bad news, he shrugged and passed the buck. That's poor leadership. Good leaders own the message. Do you believe in what you are delivering? Do you sidestep difficult conversations about faith? When talking about faith with others, do you ever deal with the difficult reality of sin and judgment? Does the reality of the eternal destiny of your neighbors sink into your bones and concern you as it should? It sure doesn't alarm us as it ought to.

Does the reality of the eternal destiny of your neighbors concern you?

Second, we need prayers that our bones would rattle in concern for those who don't yet know Christ.

Third, we need prayers that we would be able to navigate conversations in love and speak difficult truths of the gospel . . . even when it's uncomfortable. As pastor Thomas Watson said, "Unless we deny our own will, we shall never do God's will."[2]

Penn Jillette, an atheist illusionist, posted a video on YouTube reflecting on an encounter with a Christian a few years back. After one of Jillette's shows, a fan introduced himself and offered Jillette a pocket-size New Testament and Psalms bearing the man's personal inscription. The giver, a businessman, came across as just a nice, ordinary guy, and Jillette was touched and appreciative.

"I've always said I don't respect people who don't proselytize," he said. "I don't respect that at all. If you believe that there is a heaven and hell, and people could be going to hell or not getting eternal life or whatever, and you think that 'Well, it's not really worth telling them this because it would make it socially awkward.' . . . How much do you have to hate somebody to not proselytize?"

If you're convinced a truck is bearing down on someone, Jillette pointed out, you should do something about it.[3] I love the consistency of his thoughts. What would Penn Jillette think of you if he were your friend?

Boldness is hard in all circumstances, perhaps most difficult in those relationships where we feel the natural window has passed. It might be a coworker you've known for years, and a faith conversation has never come up. Or maybe it's an acquaintance who made her unbelief clear early in the relationship. But if we understand ourselves as ambassadors, we recognize our calling is not set aside for the Peters and Pauls of the world. It is for each of us. We can't opt ourselves out of this identity based on personality or discomfort. A friend of ours once shared that it is his practice to ask friends to sit with him over lunch so he can share the most important thing in his life with them. He's never been refused.

The fact that Paul is asking for boldness reminds us that evangelism is not merely the gifting of the naturally bold and extroverted; it is the calling of every Christian. In 2 Corinthians 5:20, Paul explains of himself and Timothy, "We are ambassadors for Christ, God making his appeal through us." In both cases Paul links the identity of ambassadors to the proclamation of the gospel. We are an empty pipe, a delivery system. Christ has chosen to make his appeal to the world through us.

The Words

Paul also specifically asks "that words may be given to me" (Eph. 6:19). Paul knows that he needs to deliver a clear, not muddled, gospel. Do you know what the gospel is? Can you clearly explain what the good news of Jesus Christ is?

A good starting place is Paul's own definition of the gospel in his first letter to the Corinthian church:

> I would remind you, brothers, of the gospel I preached to you, which you received, in which you stand, and by which

you are being saved, if you hold fast to the word I preached to you—unless you believed in vain.

For I delivered to you as of first importance what I also received: that Christ died for our sins in accordance with the Scriptures, that he was buried, that he was raised on the third day in accordance with the Scriptures. (1 Cor. 15:1–4)

We are sinners, and our sins deserve punishment from a just and holy God. But the good news is that Christ died for our sins, as God promised from the beginning of his redemptive plan, and in doing so, he bore the judgment we deserve. The Son of God took our sins to the grave and then conquered sin and death in his resurrection. And we can receive life eternal with God when we trust in Christ's saving work for us and entrust our lives to our Creator and Savior.

We must be able to articulate the gospel clearly. Paul had no lack of clarity of what the gospel was, yet he still asks for words to say in proclaiming the gospel. Why did Paul need prayer for words? Of all people, he knew the gospel. But only Christ knows what words will land on the hearts of those who hear the gospel. Paul depends on Christ in his request for his words to be spoken in a way that connects with the hearer.

Paul knew the gospel. But only Christ knows what words will land on the hearts of those who hear the gospel.

We've met those who have great boldness in the way they communicate the good news but not much care for the person they are sharing with. When they explain the gospel, it is as if they have been wound up. The presentation goes the same way every time. But here Paul makes it clear that every person needs to hear the gospel in a way they connect with. A socially conscious, radically feminist neighbor will likely connect with the good news of the justice of a

God who cares for the poor and oppressed and will make all things right. A lapsed Catholic friend who thinks all religions are basically the same formal, stuffy moral codes will likely need to hear of the personal relationship Jesus offers in his death and resurrection. Effective ambassadors are wise as serpents but gentle as doves (Matt. 10:16).

In Chains

Paul knows his identity: He is an "ambassador in chains" (Eph. 6:20). Why? Quite simply, because he is in prison. Paul's chains are literal. This is deeply ironic. Ambassadors wield tremendous power. In fact, in the modern world, an ambassador can't be imprisoned because of his diplomatic immunity. The entire idea of being an ambassador in chains is an oxymoron: someone in an incredibly powerful position, trapped in the worst situation. It's the equivalent of Apple's CEO in a homeless shelter. Paul, although an ambassador of the Most High King, was in jail.

But Paul views his chains in a completely different way than we would expect. Paul talks about his imprisonment and chains several times in his letters, and always with a sense of joy. There is never a sense of malice or anger for his situation. One commentator gives us a powerful way of thinking: "The term 'chain' signifies among other things the (golden) adornment(s) worn around the neck and wrists by rich ladies or high ranking men. On festive occasions, ambassadors wear such chains in order to reveal the riches, power, and dignity of the government they represent. Because Paul serves Christ crucified, he considers the painful iron prison chains as most appropriate insignia for the representation of his Lord."[4]

The chains are real, but they are also figurative. We are all called to be chained ambassadors. How so? We are sent by Jesus Christ and also chained by Jesus Christ. We are servants of the Most High! As we considered earlier, we celebrate that we are Jesus's slaves. We have exchanged the chains of our flesh for the chains of Christ. We are his bondservants, delighted with our Master.

"Declare [the mystery of the gospel] boldly," Paul says. Why? Because you are an ambassador. You are a citizen of heaven, and as such, an ambassador of the eternal kingdom on this side of eternity. Declare it boldly. Why? Because you are in chains. You have been bought with a price.

Navigating an Alien Country

Paul tells us we are aliens in this world (Eph. 2:19). We do not belong. We are made for a better, heavenly country (Heb. 11:16). When I was slogging my way through the challenges of middle school, I remember high school acquaintances telling me of the joys of the better land that awaited me. In that land, I wouldn't be the butt of every joke. I didn't need to conform to the land I lived in; I would find my kind in high school. They were right. There was something better ahead for me. Just as those high schoolers encouraged me, we get to invite others out of the twisted world we live in and into a kingdom made right. In the meantime, we look to God to provide heavenly equipment for the battles we face (Eph. 6:10–20). Only then can we represent Jesus in truth and love.

We are released by our missional Lord, who sends us out with a message of good news. We are also chained by our missional Lord— chained as his servants to this high calling. We speak the gospel because we're released to do so and because we can do nothing else. It is our obligation.

Jesus's final call to us is this: "You will receive power when the Holy Spirit has come upon you, and you will be my witnesses in Jerusalem and in all Judea and Samaria, and to the end of the earth" (Acts 1:8).

We get to be God's witnesses! It's perhaps the most important reason that Christ leaves us on earth. Patriotism promises belonging.

It promises that we can feel part of something bigger, with the hope of being part of a winning team. Yet every earthly kingdom has fallen or will fall. Every nation has been undone by the selfishness, shortsightedness, greed, or pride of its leaders. We get to belong to "a kingdom that cannot be shaken" (Heb. 12:28), and the King of Kings and Lord of Lords to whom we bow is altogether good and always working for our good. What could be better than being a citizen and ambassador of that King and kingdom?

We are released by our missional Lord, who sends us out with a message of good news.

So let us be the megaphones we are called to be. Are we people pleasers? Are our actions influenced by our fear of what others think of us? In those spaces, we choose to worship people, and we put ourselves on our own throne with a false sense of self-protection. This is a rejection of Jesus. Simply put, it is idolatry that leads to death. When our patriotism in this world is ultimate, we have placed our trust in people. We ask them to protect us, fulfill us, and give us what we need. We take on our political party's beliefs. We do what their partisan agenda says is best for the country instead of what is best, period. When we stifle the good news God has given us to declare as ambassadors, we choose to bow to our fear of people and not honor the King.

We are in allegiance either to God or to man. There is no spiritual Switzerland. Do you tend to water down the truth because you are uncomfortable with the message our Lord has given you? Lean into whom Christ has called you to be: an ambassador. Be proud of the One you represent. It brings him glory, and it is all for your good.

Your job is to speak our Lord's words, not your own. You serve the King of *the* kingdom. He has called you to be his ambassador to this world. As his ambassador, you are ultimately safe. You might endure pain and loss in this life, but the kingdom you serve is eternal. Your inheritance is secure. Be proud to stand up for your King.

As good as it is to be a resident of our native countries, how much greater it is to be a resident of the kingdom of God. We have a perfect King and are citizens of a flawless kingdom. Joy of joys. And we are called proclaimers of this great kingdom. Live faithfully as a citizen of the country God has placed you in, but do not mistake your ultimate identity. Your birthright is in an eternal, unshakable, glorious kingdom. You are a citizen and an ambassador.

PRAYER

Mighty King, forgive me for making a good gift, being a citizen of this nation, into an ultimate thing. Thank you for the gift of the country I live in, but forgive me for placing my hope and identity in my country. Thank you that you have made me a citizen of your heaven. "May your kingdom come, and your will be done, on earth as it is in heaven." What an incredible calling I have to serve as your ambassador. Thank you for the responsibility you have given me to represent you to this world. Please give me boldness. Please give me words to speak. Please help me to see those you are calling me to share the gift of your kingdom with. To you, King of Kings, be all glory, and power, and wisdom, and honor, this day and every day. Amen.

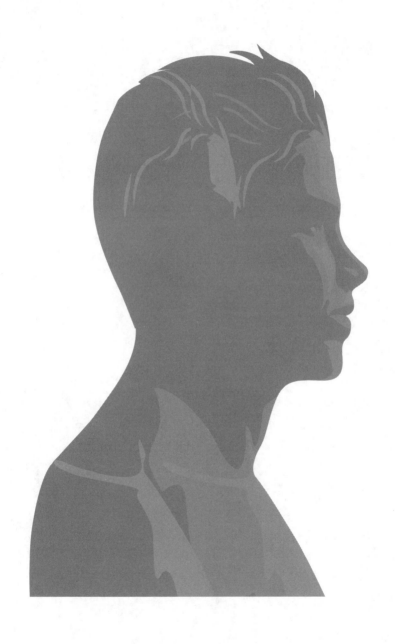

Now What?

*There are no ordinary people. You have never met a
mere mortal.*
—C. S. Lewis

*God has made his children, by adoption, nearer to him-
self than the angels. The angels are the friends of Christ;
believers are his members.*
—Thomas Watson

*Define yourself radically as one beloved by God. This is
the true self. Every other identity is illusion.*
—Brennan Manning

JOHN

TAKE A MOMENT TO TURN back to where you wrote down your answer to the question "Who are you?" from page 13. How would you
answer that question now? Pause and write down in the margin who
you now believe you are. Is your answer now more anchored? Does it
inspire hope in you? What about it brings peace to you?

We've navigated the dangers and pitfalls of various substitute identities. You know the joy of claiming your real identity. That doesn't mean it will be easy. Here are some thoughts on staying the course and some reminders of God's grace. This is your race. You can run it with the wind of the Spirit behind you, your brother Jesus at your side, and your heavenly Father in front of you.

Substitute identities cause us problems in the here and now because they draw us away from Christ. They draw us away from our Creator and whom our Creator made us to be. Are you weary? Are you tired of working so hard to become the person you thought you were hoping to be, only to be disappointed in the end?

God delighted in you when he formed you in your mother's womb. He smiled as he created you in his perfect wisdom. God knew the day of your salvation. He knew the path you would walk, the struggles you would face. And he knows who you are.

God delighted in you when he formed you in your mother's womb. He knows who you are.

God invites you not only to know but to experience who he made you to be. The journey of stepping into the true identities God has made you for is not merely knowing them in your head but receiving them in your heart. That heart knowledge not only brings peace and freedom to your spirit, but it empowers and equips you to go and be who he calls you to be.

What would it be like to go to sleep hearing the song your Father sings over you, his son? How would your prayer life change if you felt God's warm invitation to come to him as a friend to talk? How would it change your life to feel the gift of knowing you share your identity collectively with other believers as his bride, and you are not alone? What would it be like to leave your house in the morning with the clarity of purpose that comes from knowing God has appointed you as his ambassador and will send you forth in his power, not your own? Over and over in Scripture, we can hear the Lord say, "Fear not, I am with you." Living in the power of our true identities in Christ brings a profound sense of peace and rest.

The identities we've begun discovering in this book are just the start. There are far more identities that Scripture calls us to explore. You will find many of them, and a framework for understanding how they fit together, in the appendix. Perhaps we will look at those and others in another book. In the meantime, we invite you to do your own exploring.

To help you on your continued journey of understanding, it might benefit you to consider the categories of identity Christ has for us.

Born As

Every human being bears both the image of their Creator and the mark of the sin of their father, Adam. We are born as enemies of the Almighty by nature—sinners, strangers to God's promises, and slaves to this world, "having no hope and without God in the world" (Eph. 2:12). Yet every human being also carries the dignity of God and is purposed to carry out his dominion in this world. "Let us make man in our image, after our likeness" (Gen. 1:26).

Transformed Into

The journey of our identity does not end there. While we were God's enemies, he came to rescue us and make us his friends (Rom. 5:10). When we were dead, he brought us life through his death. As Paul says, "God, being rich in mercy, because of the great love with which he loved us, even when we were dead in our trespasses, made us alive together with Christ" (Eph. 2:4–5).

Those he elected, he adopted as sons, heirs of his kingdom. United with Christ, we who once were stained by sin are now saints. God is light, and that light is now in us. We are now his disciples, following the ways of Jesus, and his light shines in us. So, as we walk in this dark world, we walk as a constant source of light. And light pierces the darkness.

Included In

Christ has fashioned us into something greater than just ourselves. We are his body, with Christ Jesus our head. He is the vine; we are the branches. We are a chosen race, a holy nation. We are a city on a hill, a refuge to those in need in this wilderness. We are a holy temple for God and his dwelling place. We are Christ's bride, whom he is purifying for our wedding day. Our love will be consummated with him in eternity, where he will be our God and we will be his people.

Called To

In this world, God has great purposes for us. We are his workmanship. He has prepared good works for us from eternity. We are his ambassadors, proclaimers of his glorious kingdom on foreign soil. We intercede for those as his priests and we his servants, having no greater identity than our Master's.

Off with the Old, On with the New

When we see our identity through these lenses, we realize that nothing in our lives is *not* connected to our identity. Every activity, as mundane as it might be, has a purpose far greater than it might seem: living out our Creator's calling.

As we experience who God has made us to be, our pulses slow down, and we rest in the joy and knowledge of God's intention for our true identities in every moment.

Take off your false identities and put on your true identities.

Take off the smelly clothing of your false identities: "I am ugly," "I am worthless," "I am not enough," "I am what I do," "I am my good works," "I am a mom," "I am a dad." Throw all of them in the hamper. None of them define you. Satan is trying to destroy your life with these lies. Let Jesus's voice define you, not the Accuser's.

Put on your true identities. Jesus created you for them; he died for you so you can put them on: "I am God's image bearer," "I am beloved," "I am a treasure," "I am a sheep," "I am a son," "I am light," "I am an ambassador." Remind yourself of them when you wake up in the morning and when you go to sleep. Put reminders in your calendar and sticky notes on your dashboard. Smile, and let the lies of the world slide past as you look up at your loving Father. He has named you and knows you better than you will ever know yourself. He wants you to know him and know yourself better every day.

As Paul concludes his joyous letter to the church at Philippi, he urges them to have their thoughts reshaped by their glorious Savior. He says,

> Rejoice in the Lord always; again I will say, rejoice. Let your reasonableness be known to everyone. The Lord is at hand; do not be anxious about anything, but in everything by prayer and supplication with thanksgiving let your requests be made known to God. And the peace of God, which surpasses all understanding, will guard your hearts and your minds in Christ Jesus.
>
> Finally, brothers, whatever is true, whatever is honorable, whatever is just, whatever is pure, whatever is lovely, whatever is commendable, if there is any excellence, if there is anything worthy of praise, think about these things. What you have learned and received and heard and seen in me—practice these things, and the God of peace will be with you. (Phil. 4:4–9)

Rejoice, friends! We can set aside negative self-talk that drives us to anxiety and experience the peace of God as we lift praise to God and rest in the true, honorable, just, pure, lovely, commendable, and excellent realities of who we are in Christ Jesus.

The journey of discovering your true identities in Christ will be lifelong. We pray that God meets you on your journey. Know that we would love to hear how we can pray for you. It would be our honor to have you reach out to us at johnb@newlifetucson.com (or at my blog: thebeehive.live) and angelb@wholehopecounseling.com (or Whole Hope Biblical Counseling's website: wholehopecounseling.com).

We pray that you will know the freedom you have in Christ and that his transforming power will be manifest in you.

May he be known in you as you are known in him.

ACKNOWLEDGMENTS

THIS BOOK EMERGES FROM THE community we have been richly blessed with. To paraphrase Isaac Newton, if, by God's grace, there is fresh wisdom contained in this book, that speaks to the giants whose shoulders we rest on. We think not only of the many wise thinkers we have learned from but of the flesh and blood community we live in.

Thank you so much to every client of Whole Hope Christian Counseling who has offered us their sacred trust.

New Life Bible Fellowship, we couldn't be more grateful for you. You have loved us, trusted us, forgiven us, and extended grace upon grace to us. We are so proud of the work God is doing in your hearts. New Life staff, what an incredible team you are. We can't believe we have the blessing of working alongside you. You make our lives richer.

Stone Hill Church, thank you for being patient with us in the early years of our ministry and for generously walking alongside us even when we failed you.

To our agent, Dave Schroeder. We so appreciate your partnership and encouragement. Thank you.

To the good people at Kregel: Janyre Tromp, Rachel Kirsch, and many others. Thank you for your wisdom and for making this book significantly better.

ACKNOWLEDGMENTS

To our friends who invested hours of their time reading, editing, and providing feedback on rough early drafts, we are so grateful for your keen eyes and soft hearts that helped us shape this concept into book form.

To our moms and dads, our sisters and brothers-in-law, and all our family: Thank you for loving and supporting us. Thank you for sacrificing time with us so that we could put in the time to make this passion a reality. We couldn't imagine a more loving family. We love you.

Camille and Soren, our dearest children. You are wise beyond your years. You continue to let us into your hearts and relationships. We love you so much and are humbled to be called Mom and Dad by you two dear treasures.

Finally, and most importantly, thank you to our Creator and the one who chose us before the foundation of the world, Jesus Christ. Paraphrasing Augustine, our hearts were restless until they found their rest (and identities) in you.

Our Biblical Identities

UNDERSTANDING THE TYPES OF IDENTITIES helps the Christian form a more three-dimensional understanding of identity. If you are to ask the average Christian what their identities are in Christ, they might look quizzically at you for using the plural of identity, and then respond confidently, "Yes! I am a child of God." If we were to rank the importance of our identities in Christ, understanding our sonship might well rise to the very top, but it certainly doesn't end there. Understanding our identity in Christ solely as a child of God misses not only other identities we have been transformed into (saints, friends, citizens, etc.), but entire categories of our identities in Christ.

Many Christians tend to know who we were born as and what we were transformed into. But we often entirely miss who we are collectively and what we are called to. To that end, we are separating out four basic categories of our identities in Christ with the hope that we can rectify the profound neglect of our collective and vocational identities in Christ.

The list below is not intended to be exhaustive, but we hope that it jogs your spiritual and theological imagination and encourages you on your path of discovering who you are in Christ.

APPENDIX

Born As

*Every human bears the image of God and also
the scars of Adam's sin.*

Clay: "Has the potter no right over the clay, to make out of the same lump one vessel for honorable use and another for dishonorable use?" Romans 9:21

Darkness: "At one time you were darkness." Ephesians 5:8

Dead: "You were dead in the trespasses and sins in which you once walked." Ephesians 2:1–2

Enemy: "If while we were enemies we were reconciled to God by the death of his Son, much more, now that we are reconciled, shall we be saved by his life." Romans 5:10

Image Bearer: "Let us make man in our image, after our likeness." Genesis 1:26

Sinner: "Sin came into the world through one man, and death through sin, and so death spread to all men because all sinned." Romans 5:12

Slave: "Thanks be to God, that you who were once slaves of sin have become obedient." Romans 6:17

Steward: "Let them have dominion over the fish of the sea and over the birds of the heavens and over the livestock and over all the earth and over every creeping thing that creeps on the earth." Genesis 1:26

Stranger: "You are no longer strangers and aliens, but you are fellow citizens with the saints and members of the household of God." Ephesians 2:19

Wonderfully Made: "I praise you, for I am fearfully and wonderfully made." Psalm 139:14

APPENDIX

Transformed Into

By God's grace and through Christ's work on the cross, we are chosen as sons and transformed into the likeness of Christ through the power of the Holy Spirit.

Adopted Son: "You did not receive the spirit of slavery to fall back into fear, but you have received the Spirit of adoption as sons, by whom we cry, 'Abba! Father!'" Romans 8:15

Alive: "God, being rich in mercy, because of the great love with which he loved us, even when we were dead in our trespasses, made us alive together with Christ—by grace you have been saved." Ephesians 2:4–5

Beloved: "I have loved you with an everlasting love; therefore I have continued my faithfulness to you." Jeremiah 31:3

Blameless: "He chose us in him before the foundation of the world, that we should be holy and blameless before him." Ephesians 1:4

Blessed: "He has blessed us [with his glorious grace] in the Beloved." Ephesians 1:6

Broken Vessels: "We are afflicted in every way, but not crushed; perplexed, but not driven to despair." 2 Corinthians 4:8

Citizen: "Our citizenship is in heaven, and from it we await a Savior, the Lord Jesus Christ." Philippians 3:20

Clothed: "The angel said to those who were standing before him, 'Remove the filthy garments from him.' And to him he said, 'Behold, I have taken your iniquity away from you, and I will clothe you with pure vestments.'" Zechariah 3:4

Crucified: "We know that our old self was crucified with him in order that the body of sin might be brought to nothing, so that we would no longer be enslaved to sin." Romans 6:6

Disciple: "By this all people will know that you are my disciples, if you have love for one another." John 13:35

Forgiven: "Blessed are those whose lawless deeds are forgiven, and whose sins are covered." Romans 4:7

Free: "It is for freedom that Christ has set us free. Stand firm, then, and do not let yourselves be burdened again by a yoke of slavery." Galatians 5:1 NIV

Friend: "No longer do I call you servants, for the servant does not know what his master is doing; but I have called you friends, for all that I have heard from my Father I have made known to you." John 15:15

God's Workmanship: "We are his workmanship, created in Christ Jesus for good works, which God prepared beforehand, that we should walk in them." Ephesians 2:10

Heir: "If [we are] children, then heirs—heirs of God and fellow heirs with Christ." Romans 8:17

In Christ: "There is therefore now no condemnation for those who are in Christ Jesus." Romans 8:1

Indwelt by the Holy Spirit: "You, however, are not in the flesh but in the Spirit, if in fact the Spirit of God dwells in you. Anyone who does not have the Spirit of Christ does not belong to him." Romans 8:9

Justified: "You were washed, you were sanctified, you were justified in the name of the Lord Jesus Christ and by the Spirit of our God." 1 Corinthians 6:11

Minister: "Our sufficiency is from God, who has made us sufficient to be ministers of a new covenant." 2 Corinthians 3:5–6

More than a Conqueror: "In all these things we are more than conquerors through him who loved us." Romans 8:37

Newborn: "Jesus answered, 'Truly, truly, I say to you, unless one is born of water and the Spirit, he cannot enter the kingdom of God.'" John 3:5

New Creation: "If anyone is in Christ, he is a new creation. The old has passed away; behold, the new has come." 2 Corinthians 5:17

APPENDIX

Overcomer: "Everyone who has been born of God overcomes the world. And this is the victory that has overcome the world—our faith." 1 John 5:4

Predestined: "Those whom he foreknew he also predestined to be conformed to the image of his Son, in order that he might be the firstborn among many brothers." Romans 8:29

Protected: "Holy Father, keep them in your name, which you have given me, that they may be one, even as we are one." John 17:11

Purchased: "You are not your own, for you were bought with a price. So glorify God in your body." 1 Corinthians 6:19–20

Reigning: "If, because of one man's trespass, death reigned through that one man, much more will those who receive the abundance of grace and the free gift of righteousness reign in life through the one man Jesus Christ." Romans 5:17

Resurrected: "If we have been united with him in a death like his, we shall certainly be united with him in a resurrection like his." Romans 6:5

Righteousness: "For our sake he made him to be sin who knew no sin, so that in him we might become the righteousness of God." 2 Corinthians 5:21

Saint: "Paul, an apostle of Christ Jesus by the will of God, to the saints who are in Ephesus, and are faithful in Christ Jesus." Ephesians 1:1

Seated in the Heavenly Realms: "[God] raised us up with him [Christ] and seated us with him in the heavenly places in Christ Jesus." Ephesians 2:6

Secure: "I give them [my sheep] eternal life, and they will never perish, and no one will snatch them out of my hand." John 10:28

Set Apart: "If anyone cleanses himself from what is dishonorable, he will be a vessel for honorable use, set apart as holy, useful to the master of the house, ready for every good work." 2 Timothy 2:21

Sheep: "The LORD is my shepherd; I shall not want." Psalm 23:1

Soldier: "Finally, be strong in the Lord and in the strength of his might. Put on the whole armor of God, that you may be able to stand against the schemes of the devil." Ephesians 6:10–11

Treasure: "When she has found it, she calls together her friends and neighbors, saying, 'Rejoice with me, for I have found the coin that I had lost.' Just so, I tell you, there is joy before the angels of God over one sinner who repents." Luke 15:9–10

Included In

God adopts us into a family that together radiates the light of Christ to the world and is his dwelling place.

Aroma of Christ: "We are the aroma of Christ to God among those who are being saved and among those who are perishing, to one a fragrance from death to death, to the other a fragrance from life to life." 2 Corinthians 2:15–16

Body: "In one Spirit we were all baptized into one body—Jews or Greeks, slaves or free—and all were made to drink of one Spirit." 1 Corinthians 12:13

Branches: "I am the vine; you are the branches. Whoever abides in me and I in him, he it is that bears much fruit, for apart from me you can do nothing." John 15:5

Bride: "I saw the holy city, new Jerusalem, coming down out of heaven from God, prepared as a bride adorned for her husband." Revelation 21:2

Chosen Race: "You are a chosen race, a royal priesthood, a holy nation, a people for his own possession, that you may proclaim the excellencies of him who called you out of darkness into his marvelous light." 1 Peter 2:9

APPENDIX

City on a Hill: "A city set on a hill cannot be hidden." Matthew 5:14

Dwelling Place: "In him you also are being built together into a dwelling place for God by the Spirit." Ephesians 2:22

Exiles: "If you call on him as Father who judges impartially according to each one's deeds, conduct yourselves with fear throughout the time of your exile." 1 Peter 1:17

Gifted: "To each is given the manifestation of the Spirit for the common good." 1 Corinthians 12:7

Holy Nation: "You are a chosen race, a royal priesthood, a holy nation, a people for his own possession, that you may proclaim the excellencies of him who called you out of darkness into his marvelous light." 1 Peter 2:9

Light: "You are the light of the world." Matthew 5:14

Members of a Body: "We, though many, are one body in Christ, and individually members one of another." Romans 12:5

New Jerusalem: "I saw the holy city, new Jerusalem, coming down out of heaven from God, prepared as a bride adorned for her husband." Revelation 21:2

One: "Holy Father, keep them in your name, which you have given me, that they may be one, even as we are one." John 17:11

Salt: "You are the salt of the earth." Matthew 5:13

Sojourners: "Beloved, I urge you as sojourners and exiles to abstain from the passions of the flesh, which wage war against your soul." 1 Peter 2:11

Temple: "Do you not know that you are God's temple and that God's Spirit dwells in you?" 1 Corinthians 3:16

United: "I appeal to you, brothers, by the name of our Lord Jesus Christ, that all of you agree, and that there be no divisions among you, but that you be united in the same mind and the same judgment." 1 Corinthians 1:10

Called To

God has a calling on our lives for the purpose of the advancement of his kingdom.

Ambassador: "Therefore, we are ambassadors for Christ, God making his appeal through us." 2 Corinthians 5:20

Farmer: "I planted, Apollos watered, but God gave the growth." 1 Corinthians 3:6

Fisher: "Follow me, and I will make you fishers of men." (Matt. 4:19)

Laborer: "I heard a voice from heaven saying, 'Write this: Blessed are the dead who die in the Lord from now on.' 'Blessed indeed,' says the Spirit, 'that they may rest from their labors, for their deeds follow them!'" Revelation 14:13

Priest: "You are a chosen race, a royal priesthood, a holy nation, a people for his own possession, that you may proclaim the excellencies of him who called you out of darkness into his marvelous light." 1 Peter 2:9

Servant: "This is how one should regard us, as servants of Christ and stewards of the mysteries of God." 1 Corinthians 4:1

Slave: "But now . . . you have been set free from sin and have become slaves of God." Romans 6:22

Workers: "We are God's fellow workers." 1 Corinthians 3:9

NOTES

The Elusive Search

1. Stephen Barker, "9 Times Daniel Day-Lewis Took Method Acting to the Extreme," *Screen Rant*, February 6, 2022, https://screenrant.com/daniel-day-lewis-wild-method-acting-stories.

2. Josh Hafner, "Surgeon General: 1 in 7 in USA Will Face Substance Addiction," *USA Today*, November 17, 2016, https://www.usatoday.com/story/news/nation-now/2016/11/17/surgeon-general-1-7-us-face-substance-addiction/93993474.

3. "The Science Behind Positive Affirmations," Third Space, *This Space*, February 4, 2021, https://www.thirdspace.london/this-space/2021/02/the-science-behind-positive-affirmations.

4. Eugene H. Peterson, *Run with the Horses: The Quest for Life at Its Best*, commemorative ed. (Downers Grove, IL: IVP Books, 2019), 37–38.

Mask 1: Shame

1. Lea Winerman, "By the Numbers: An Alarming Rise in Suicide," *Monitor on Psychology* 50, no. 1 (January 2019): 1, https://www.apa.org/monitor/2019/01/numbers.

2. Laura Santhanam, "Youth Suicide Rates Are on the Rise in the U.S.," *PBS News Hour*, October 18, 2019, https://www.pbs.org/newshour/health/youth-suicide-rates-are-on-the-rise-in-the-u-s.

3. Rosemary Sedgwick et al., "Social Media, Internet Use and Suicide Attempts in Adolescents," *Current Opinion in Psychiatry* 32, no. 6 (November 2019): 534–41, https://journals.lww.com/co-psychiatry/fulltext/2019/11000/social_media,_internet_use_and_suicide_attempts_in.12.aspx.

4. Curt Thompson, *The Soul of Shame: Retelling the Stories We Believe About Ourselves* (Downers Grove, IL: IVP Books, 2015), 186.

5. *The Help*, directed by Tate Taylor, featuring Viola Davis (Universal City, CA: DreamWorks Pictures, 2011).

6. Despite most depictions, the Romans would not have been delicate enough to cover Jesus with a loincloth. His nakedness was part of his humiliation.

7. Dane Ortlund, *Gentle and Lowly: The Heart of Christ for Sinners and Sufferers* (Wheaton, IL: Crossway, 2020), 179.

8. Thompson, *The Soul of Shame*, 176.

9. Thompson, *The Soul of Shame*, 186.

Mask 2: Good Works

1. David Zahl, *Seculosity: How Career, Parenting, Technology, Food, Politics, and Romance Became Our New Religion and What to Do About It* (Minneapolis: Fortress, 2019), 6.

2. Zahl, *Seculosity*, xiv, emphasis in original.

3. *Rocketman*, directed by Dexter Fletcher, featuring Kit Connor (Los Angeles: Paramount Pictures, 2019).

4. "Creep," track 2 on Radiohead, *Pablo Honey*, Parlophone, 1993.

5. Michael Smith, "Studies Show that Children Just Want to Be Famous," *Liberty Voice*, August 3, 2013, https://guardianlv.com/2013/08/studies-show-that-children-just-want-to-be-famous.

6. Gaby Del Valle, "Millennials Prioritize Owning a Home over Getting Married or Having Kids," *Vox*, October 10, 2018,

https://www.vox.com/the-goods/2018/10/10/17959808/millen
nial-homeownership-student-loans-rent-burden.

7. Thomas Watson, *The Beatitudes: An Exposition of Matthew 5:1–12*, first published 1660, Grace-eBooks, https://www.grace
-ebooks.com/library/Thomas%20Watson/TW_The%20Beati
tudes.pdf, 37.

8. Thomas DeWitt Talmage, *The Pathway of Life* (Philadelphia: Historical Publishing Company, 1894), 249.

9. Thomas Boston, *The Crook in the Lot: The Sovereignty and Wisdom of God Displayed in the Affliction of Men*, A Puritan's Mind, accessed December 13, 2022, https://www.apuritans
mind.com/arminianism/the-crook-in-the-lot-by-thomas-bos
ton.

10. *Saturday Night Live*, season 44, episode 19, "Romano Tours," written by Anna Drezen and Alison Gates, featuring Adam Sandler, aired May 4, 2019, on NBC, https://www.youtube
.com/watch?v=TbwlC2B-BIg.

11. *Saturday Night Live*, season 17, episode 7, "Daily Affirmations: Dysfunctional Family," written by Al Franken, featuring Al Franken and Macaulay Culkin, aired November 23, 1991, on NBC, https://www.youtube.com/watch?v=G8DVe5hNpBE.

12. Timothy Keller with Kathy Keller, *The Meaning of Marriage: Facing the Complexities of Commitment with the Wisdom of God* (New York: Riverhead Books, 2011), 44.

13. Saint Augustine, *City of God*, ed. Vernon J. Bourke (New York: Image, 1958), bk. IV, ch. III.

Mask 3: Independence

1. I (John) fully own my responsibility in not protecting and caring for Angel as I should have in the early years of ministry. I share more about that in chapters 6 and 9. We are working on a forthcoming book that will share the fullness of the story of

our broken and restored marriage. If you are fighting through hurt in your marriage, take heart—our God loves reconciling.

2. Brian Mazique, "Michael Jordan's High School Coach Exposes Another MJ Myth," Bleacher Report, January 11, 2012, https://bleacherreport.com/articles/1020151-michael-jordans-high-school-coach-exposes-another-mj-myth.

3. "Lady Gaga," Biography, April 4, 2022, https://www.biography.com/musicians/lady-gaga.

4. "About," JKRowling.com, accessed March 7, 2023, https://www.jkrowling.com/about.

5. Barry Schwartz, "More Isn't Always Better," *Harvard Business Review*, June 2006, https://hbr.org/2006/06/more-isnt-always-better.

6. Adam Gabbatt, "Losing Their Religion: Why US Churches Are on the Decline," *The Guardian*, January 22, 2023, https://www.theguardian.com/us-news/2023/jan/22/us-churches-closing-religion-covid-christianity.

7. J. Maureen Henderson, "One in Four Millennials Would Quit Their Job to Be Famous," *Forbes*, January 24, 2017, https://www.forbes.com/sites/jmaureenhenderson/2017/01/24/one-in-four-millennials-would-quit-their-job-to-be-famous/#2f8d8ecf2c43.

8. Henry Austin Dobson, "Fame Is a Food that Dead Men Eat," *All Poetry*, accessed March 7, 2022, https://allpoetry.com/fame-is-a-food-that-dead-men-eat.

9. "Strong's G1401 - *duolos*," Blue Letter Bible, https://www.blueletterbible.org/lexicon/g1401.

10. For instance, see Exod. 12:43–44; 21:2, 20–27; Lev. 25:6, 46; Deut. 24:7; Jer. 34:8–10.

11. Angela Duckworth, *Grit: The Power of Passion and Perseverance* (New York: Scribner, 2016), 149.

NOTES

Mask 4: Individuality

1. It's worth noting that there is some concern in Christian circles regarding the origins of some personality type testing, including the Enneagram. Navigating those issues is beyond the purview of this chapter.

2. "CliftonStrengths," Gallup, accessed June 20, 2022, https://www.gallup.com/cliftonstrengths/en/254033/strengthsfinder.aspx.

3. Ian Morgan Cron and Suzanne Stabile, *The Road Back to You: An Enneagram Journey to Self-Discovery* (Downers Grove, IL: IVP Books, 2016), 23.

4. Amy Hwang, "My Personality Type," *New Yorker*, January 30, 2023, https://condenaststore.com/featured/my-personality-type-amy-hwang.html

5. Frederick Buechner, *Telling Secrets: A Memoir* (New York: HarperCollins, 1991), 45.

6. Alan Cassels, *Ideology and International Relations in the Modern World* (New York: Routledge, 1996), 159.

7. Harold Senkbeil, *The Care of Souls: Cultivating a Pastor's Heart* (Bellingham, WA: Lexham Press, 2019), 225.

8. These are Enneagram types.

9. Max Lucado has a beautiful reflection on truths that emerge from Psalm 23 in his book *Traveling Light: Releasing the Burdens You Were Never Intended to Bear* (Nashville: Thomas Nelson, 2001).

Mask 5: Desires

1. See *Why Does God Care Who I Sleep With?* by Sam Allberry, *Washed and Waiting* by Wesley Hill, or *What Does the Bible Really Teach About Homosexuality?* by Kevin DeYoung for much fuller accounts of what the Bible teaches regarding sexuality.

2. The word *Christian*, by the way, only appears seven times in the Bible, in contrast to the numerous times *saints* is used in reference to believers.

3. Kelly M. Kapic, *A Little Book for New Theologians: Why and How to Study Theology* (Downers Grove, IL: IVP Academic, 2012), 46.

4. Saint Augustine, *The Confessions of Saint Augustine*, trans. John K. Ryan (New York: Doubleday, 1960), 1.

5. Augustine, *Confessions*, 163.

Mask 6: Marriage

1. *Jerry Maguire*, directed by Cameron Crowe (Culver City, CA: TriStar Pictures, 1996).

2. Eli J. Finkel, *The All-or-Nothing Marriage: How the Best Marriages Work* (New York: Dutton, 2017), chaps. 2–4.

3. Timothy Keller with Kathy Keller, *The Meaning of Marriage: Facing the Complexities of Commitment with the Wisdom of God* (New York: Riverhead Books, 2011), 118, emphasis in original.

4. Frank Newport, "2017 Update on Americans and Religion," Gallup, December 22, 2017, https://news.gallup.com/poll/2246 42/2017-update-americans-religion.aspx.

5. Rachel Paul, Jesse Sharrard, and Song Xiong, "The Importance of Face-to-Face Communication in the Digital World," *Society for Nutrition Education and Behavior* 48, no. 10 (November 1, 2016): 681, https://doi.org/10.1016/j.jneb.2016.09.014.

6. Jeremy Weber, "Pew: Why Americans Go to Church or Stay Home," *Christianity Today*, August 1, 2018, https://www.chris tianitytoday.com/news/2018/july/church-attendance-top-rea sons-go-or-stay-home-pew.html.

7. See "The State of the Church 2016," Barna Group, September 15, 2016, https://www.barna.com/research/state-church-2016.

If you lower the threshold to attending once a month, the number rises to 50 percent. Emma Green, "It's Hard to Go to Church," *The Atlantic*, August 23, 2016, https://www.the atlantic.com/politics/archive/2016/08/religious-participation -survey/496940. However, both numbers are self-reported and thus are almost certainly lower.

8. Our numbers were arrived at by computing Tucson's population and dividing it by the number of churches in Tucson (of all types) and their average size. Our numbers have been confirmed externally by *4 Tucson*.

9. The number of those who attend church regularly is around twice those in attendance on any given weekend, so the likely number of regular attenders in Tucson is about 6 percent.

10. "What Americans Know About Religion," Pew Research Center, July 23, 2019, https://www.pewresearch.org/religion/2019 /07/23/what-americans-know-about-religion.

11. *2020 State of American Theology Study*, LifeWay Research, accessed August 27, 2022, http://research.lifeway.com/wp-content /uploads/2020/09/Ligonier-State-of-Theology-2020-White-Pa per.pdf.

12. Weber, "Pew: Why Americans Go to Church or Stay Home."

13. The only letter that is an exception is Philemon. Revelation is apocalyptic literature, but it is also John's letter to seven churches.

14. Curt Parton, "Just How Big Were the Early House Churches?" *Exploring the Faith*, July 2, 2019, https://exploringthefaith .com/2019/07/02/just-how-big-were-the-early-house-churches.

15. The earliest house church that has been excavated (in the ancient village of Dura Europos in modern Syria) is thought to have been active in the early third century and has a baptismal font and beautiful frescoes throughout. See J. P. Mauro, "These Frescoes Adorned the Oldest Extant Christian House

Church," Aleteia, May 1, 2021, https://aleteia.org/2021/05/01/these-frescoes-adorned-the-oldest-extant-christian-house-church.

16. Aaron Earls, "Small Churches Continue Growing—But in Number, Not Size," Lifeway Research, October 20, 2021, https://research.lifeway.com/2021/10/20/small-churches-continue-growing-but-in-number-not-size.

17. See Revelation 5, 7, and 19.

18. D. A. Carson, *Love in Hard Places* (Wheaton, IL: Crossway, 2002), 61.

19. Dietrich Bonhoeffer, *Dietrich Bonhoeffer Works, Volume 5: Life Together, Prayerbook of the Bible*, trans. Daniel W. Bloesch and James H. Burtness (Minneapolis: Fortress, 2005), 97–98.

20. Irenaeus, *Against Heresies*, in vol. 1 of *Ante-Nicene Fathers*, ed. Alexander Roberts (Baltimore: Veritatis Splendor Publications, 2012), III.4.

21. Origen, *The Fathers of the Church: Origen: Homilies on Joshua*, trans. Barbara J. Bruce, ed. Cynthia White (Washington, DC: The Catholic University of America Press, 2002), 50.

22. Cyprian of Carthage, "Epistle 72," Church Fathers, accessed January 26, 2023, www.newadvent.org/fathers/050671.htm.

23. This does not mean that we take responsibility that isn't ours. Christ is the Groom, not us. For some of us in vocational ministry this can be a challenge. John's heart breaks when he reflects on the pain he caused me in the early years of ministry when he hadn't yet learned that lesson. "I took on a new wife when I began serving as a pastor," John confesses.

Mask 7: Parenthood

1. Louie Giglio, "The Perfect Father," sermon, Passion City

Church, Atlanta, GA, posted May 7, 2019, 19:12, https://www .youtube.com/watch?v=mEmPzFgtnCY.

2. Eric Geiger, *Identity: Who You Are in Christ* (Nashville: B&H Publishing, 2008), 29–32.

3. Mark Buchanan, *The Holy Wild: Trusting in the Character of God* (Colorado Springs: Multnomah, 2003), 84.

4. In Numbers 27, before Israel entered the promised land, God made a provision for inheritance by daughters in certain circumstances.

5. For instance, see Romans 8:14, "For all who are led by the Spirit of God are sons of God." Or Galatians 3:26, "For in Christ Jesus you are all sons of God, through faith." Or Hebrews 12:7, "God is treating you as sons."

6. Paul E. Miller, *A Praying Life: Connecting with God in a Distracting World* (Colorado Springs: NavPress, 2009), 39.

7. Dietrich Bonhoeffer, *The Cost of Discipleship* (New York: Touchstone, 1995), 304.

8. Larry Hurtado, *Destroyer of the gods: Early Christian Distinctiveness in the Roman World* (Waco, TX: Baylor University Press, 2016).

Mask 8: Ideologies

1. Wendy Wang, "Marriages Between Democrats and Republicans Are Extremely Rare," Institute for Family Studies, November 3, 2020, https://ifstudies.org/blog/marriages-between -democrats-and-republicans-are-extremely-rare.

2. Wang, "Marriages Between Democrats and Republicans."

3. "A Country Divided: 10 Per Cent of American Couples Have Ended a Relationship Because of Political Differences," *The Daily Mail*, May 10, 2017, https://www.dailymail.co.uk/news

/article-4493726/Donald-Trump-s-win-causing-couples-split
.html.

4. Seán Clarke, "Changing Attitudes to Brexit, Three Years On," *The Guardian*, January 30, 2023, https://www.theguardian .com/politics/ng-interactive/2023/jan/30/changing-attitudes -to-brexit-three-years-on; Ana Gonzalez-Barrera and Phillip Connor, "Around the World, More Say Immigrants Are a Strength Than a Burden," Pew Research Center, March 14, 2019, https://www.pewresearch.org/global/2019/03/14/around -the-world-more-say-immigrants-are-a-strength-than-a-bur den; Sook Jong Lee, "Generational Divides and the Future of South Korean Democracy," Carnegie Endowment for International Peace, June 29, 2021, https://carnegieendowment.org /2021/06/29/generational-divides-and-future-of-south-korean -democracy-pub-84818.

5. Brant Hansen, *Unoffendable: How Just One Change Can Make All of Life Better* (Nashville: W Publishing, 2015), 125.

6. Timothy and Kathy Keller reflect on this powerful truth in *The Meaning of Marriage: Facing the Complexities of Commitment with the Wisdom of God* (New York: Riverhead Books, 2011), 101.

7. Ken Sande, *The Peacemaker* (Grand Rapids, MI: Baker Books, 2004), 22. Sande says, "Conflict is an opportunity to solve common problems in a way that honors God and offers benefits to those involved."

8. Keller, *Meaning of Marriage*, 122.

9. Andrée Seu Peterson, "Depth Perception and Marriage," *The World and Everything in It*, WORLD Radio, July 7, 2019, https://worldandeverything.org/2019/07/andree-sue-peterson -depth-perception-and-marriage.

10. Michelle Christy, "Mary and Martha: Sitting at the Feet of

Jesus," Faithward, accessed March 3, 2023, https://www
.faithward.org/women-of-the-bible-study-series/mary-and
-martha-sitting-at-the-feet-of-jesus.

Mask 9: Career

1. "What Percentage of the Average Life of an American Is Spent in School?" Reference, April 3, 2020, https://www.reference .com/world-view/percentage-average-life-american-spent -school-b4bf5e983cdb6f65. In addition to the investment in time is the financial investment. School costs $12,612 a year per pupil (for public education). That puts even just the high school graduate's investment at over $150,000 and the college graduate of even an in-state university at over $200,000. Once you graduate and move into your career, then the true investment begins. "Per Pupil Spending by State 2023," World Review, accessed March 3, 2023, https://worldpopulationreview .com/state-rankings/per-pupil-spending-by-state.

2. "One Third of Your Life Is Spent at Work," *Gettysburg College News*, accessed March 3, 2022, https://www.gettysburg.edu /news/stories?id=79db7b34-630c-4f49-ad32-4ab9ea48e72b.

3. Charles Spurgeon, "Foretastes of the Heavenly Life," Sermons and Biblical Studies, Biblia.Work, accessed March 3, 2022, https://www.biblia.work/sermons/foretastes-of-the-heavenly -life. Originally delivered in the New Park Street Chapel, Southwark, England, 1857.

4. If you need help discovering your spiritual gifts, we recommend the S.H.A.P.E. assessment, which can be found at https:// www.freeshapetest.com.

Mask 10: Patriotism

1. Stephen Burgen, "Spain Sacks Ambassador to Belgium for

'Absenteeism and Abuse of Power,'" *The Guardian*, April 9, 2016, https://www.theguardian.com/world/2016/apr/09/spain -sacks-ambassador-ignacio-matellanes-martinez-belgium -failing-to-represent-country.

2. Thomas Watson, *The Thomas Watson Collection* (Cudahy, WI: First Rate Publishers, 2014), 613.

3. Penn Jillette, "A Gift of a Bible," posted July 8, 2010, You-Tube video, 3:00, https://www.youtube.com/watch?v=6md638 smQd8.

4. Markus Barth, *Ephesians 4–6: A New Translation with Introduction and Commentary*, Anchor Bible (New Haven, CT: Yale University Press, 1998), 782.26.